Answer Key for Harvey's Revised English Grammar

Answers and teaching helps by
Eric E. Wiggin, M.S. Ed.

editor of *Harvey's Elementary Grammar and Composition*
and *Harvey's Revised English Grammar*

All Scriptures are from the King James Version of the Bible.

Copyright © 1987 by Mott Media

All rights in this book are reserved. No portion of this book may be reproduced by any process such as mimeograph, photocopying, recording, storage in a retrieval or transmitted by any means without written permission of the publisher. Brief quotations embodied in critical articles or reviews are permitted. For information write Mott Media, 1000 E. Huron, Milford, Michigan 48042.

LIBRARY OF CONGRESS CATALOGING IN PUBLICATION DATA

Wiggen, Eric E.
   Answer key for Harvey's revised English grammar.

   1. Harvey, Thomas W. (Thomas Wadleigh), 1821?-1892. Revised English grammar. 2. English language—Grammar— Study and teaching—Aids and devices. I. Harvey, Thomas W. (Thomas Wadleigh), 1821?-1892. Revised English grammar. II. Title.

PE1111.H4703W54   1987   428.2   87-31404

ISBN 0-88062-154-0 (pbk.)

Answer Key and Teaching Aids for Harvey's Revised English Grammar

Pages 9-10

11-12. CAPITAL LETTERS/EXERCISES
   1. It . . . . Man . . . . Flowers . . . .
   2. That . . . Constitution.
   3. For . . . . For
   4. You . . . . A . . . .
   5. The . . . O . . . /The . . . .
   6. Samuel . . . Baltimore . . . General Assembly . . . Monday . . . February.
   7. President . . . Esq . . . . Third . . . Lord (**Opposition** may be capitalized if it refers to a particular political party, as; Her Majesty's loyal **Opposition**).
   8. Music . . . .
   9. Central Park . . . River . . . Great Expectations . . . Atlas Mountains . . . .
  10. Lord (or **LORD**, if quoted from the King James Bible) . . . Creator . . . Providence.
  11. Word (**Redeemer, Way, Truth,** and **Life,** since they appear as quotes from the K.J. Bible, should not be capitalized. As descriptive terms, rather than strictly names for deity, the translators treat them as common nouns, and **in quotations** from the K.J.V., therefore, they must be written in lower case. In non-quoted allusions to God they are often capitalized, however).
  12. Chinese . . . Turkomans. . . Indians (**Gypsy** is capitalized only when it refers to their language, Romany).
  13. Swiss Family . . . Russian . . . guinea . . . Cashmere . . . damask (**Guinea** is here lower case, since it refers to a gold coin; likewise with **guinea** fowl/pig, which have become common; **Guinea**, the African country, is capitalized, and so are its products, as; **Guinea** corn. **Cashmere**, likewise, is not capitalized, except when it retains its original spelling, Kashmir. Students should be expected to research these rules in their dictionaries).
  14. Emancipation Proclamation. . . The Art of Cookery . . . Compromise . . . Whiskey Insurrection . . . Treatise . . . Science . . . Education . . . Art . . . Teaching.
  15. I . . . . I . . . . Oh . . . I . . . .

Page 13

15. MODELS FOR ANALYZING SYLLABLES
Analyze the following:

  And—a syllable containing three elementary sounds.
  A—a vowel-vocal, short sound.
  n—a consonant-subvocal-linguo-nasal.
  d—a consonant-linguo-dental.
  Fly—a syllable containing three elementary sounds.
  F—a consonant-aspirate-labial.
  l—a consonant-subvocal-lingual.
  y—a vowel-vocal, long sound.
  Warm—a syllable containing four elementary sounds.
  W—a consonant-subvocal-labial.
  a—a vowel-vocal, middle sound.
  r—a consonant-subvocal-lingual.
  m—a consonant-subvocal-labial.
  Elm—a syllable containing three elementary sounds.
  E—a vowel-vocal, short sound.
  l—a consonant-subvocal-lingual.
  m—a consonant-subvocal-labial.
  Fin—a syllable containing three elementary sounds.
  F—a consonant aspirate-labial.
  i—a vowel, vocal, short sound.
  n—a consonant-subvocal-linguo-nasal.
  Sing—a syllable containing three elementary sounds.
  S—a consonant-linguo-dental.
  i—a vowel-vocal, short sound.
  ng—a consonant-subvocal-palato-nasal.
  Wax—a syllable containing four elementary sounds.
  W—a consonant-subvocal-labial.
  a—a vowel-vocal, short sound.
  x—a substitute for ks.
  k—a consonant-aspirate-palatal.
  s—a consonant-aspirate-linguo-dental.
  When—a syllable containing three elementary sounds.
  Wh—a consonant-aspirate-labial.
  e—a vowel-vocal, short sound.
  n—a consonant-subvocal-linguo-nasal.
  Sue—a syllable containing two elementary sounds.
  S—a consonant-aspirate-linguo-dental.
  ue—a digraph, equivalent to **u long**.

PAGE 13-14

Light—a syllable containing three elementary sounds.
   L—a consonant-subvocal-lingual.
   i—a vowel-vocal, long sound.
   gh—silent letters. They have no sound.
   t—a consonant-aspirate-linguo-dental.

Pot—a syllable containing three elementary sounds.
   P—a consonant-aspirate-labial.
   o—a vowel-vocal, short sound.
   t—a consonant-aspirate-linguo-dental.

Home—a syllable containing three elementary sounds.
   H—a consonant-aspirate-palatal.
   o—a vowel-vocal, long sound.
   m—a consonant-subvocal-labial.
   e—silent; it has no sound.

Zinc—a syllable containing four elementary sounds.
   Z—a consonant-subvocal-linguo-dental.
   i—a vowel-vocal, short sound.
   n—a consonant-subvocal-palatal-nasal substitute.
   c—a consonant-aspirate-palatal substitute for k.

Valve—a syllable containing three elementary sounds.
   V—(both positions)—a consonant-subvocal-labial.
   a—a vowel-vocal, short sound.
   l—a consonant-subvocal-lingual.
   e—a silent letter.

Kid—a syllable containing three elementary sounds.
   K—a consonant-aspirate-palatal.
   i—a vowel-vocal, short sound.
   d—a consonant-subvocal-linguo-dental.

Ask—a syllable containing three elementary sounds.
   A—a vowel-vocal, Italian sound.
   s—a consonant-aspirate-linguo-dental.
   k—a consonant-aspirate-palatal.

Sun—a syllable containing three elementary sounds.
   S—a consonant-aspirate-linguo-dental.
   u—a vowel-vocal, short sound.
   n—a consonant-subvocal-linguo-nasal.

Goat—a syllable containing three elementary sounds.
   oa—a vowel-vocal, long sound, substitute for **o**, as in **cold**.
   t—a consonant-aspirate-linguo-dental.

Jolt—a syllable containing four elementary sounds.
   J—a consonant-subvocal-linguo-dental.
   o—a vowel-vocal, long sound.
   l—a consonant-subvocal-lingual.
   t—a consonant-aspirate-lingual-dental.

Form syllables by prefixing a consonant to **a, ay, eau, oy** (answers may vary):
   ha, may, beau, toy.

By prefixing two or more consonants to **e, oo, ow, i**:
   pre, snoo(ze), prow, tri.

By affixing one, two or more consonants to any of the vowels or dipthongs (may be done as an oral or written exercise).

Page 14
17. MODELS FOR ANALYZING WORDS
Analyze the following words:

   Sand, lead, and **sack**—monosyllables.

   Unc ′ tion, fam ′ ous, great ′ ly—all dissyllables, accented on the first syllable.

   En dea ′ vor—a trisyllable, accented on the second syllable.

   Can ′ did ly—trisyllable, first.

   Un ′ pop ′ u lar—four syllables, polysyllable; secondary, first; primary, second.

   In ′ for ma ′ tion—four syllables, polysyllable; secondary first; primary, third.

   Gra tu ′ i tous—four syllables, polysyllable; accent on the second.

   Do mes ′ ti ca ′ tion—five syllables, polysyllable; secondary, second; primary, fourth.

   In terr ′ o ga ′ tion—five syllables, polysyllable; secondary, second; primary, fourth.

   In ′ cre du ′ li ty—five syllables, polysyllable; secondary, first; primary, third.

   In ′ com pre hen ′ si ble—six syllables, polysyllable; secondary, first; primary, fourth.

   In ′ de fen ′ si ble ness—six syllables, polysyllable; secondary, first; primary, third.

   In ′ com pass ′ ion ate ly—six syllables, polysyllable; secondary, first; primary, third.

Correct the accent:
   Ad ′ ver tise ′ ment
   Pri ′ ma ′ ry
   Con ′ tra ′ ry
   Leg ′ is la ′ ture
   La ′ men ta ble or **la men ′ ta ble**
   Sec ′ on dar ′ y
   In ′ fa mous
   Ar ′ mi stice
   Ad ′ mir a ble
   In ′ ter es ting
   In ′ sult—a rude act or remark.
   In sult ′—verb; to be rude.
   Fer ′ ment—noun; substance causing fermentation.

Fer ment′—verb; to cause or undergo fermentation.
Reb′ **el**—noun; one who revolts.
Re bel′—verb; to revolt.
Rec′ **ord**—noun; phonograph disk
Re cord′—verb; to copy.
Pre′ **lude**—noun; an introducing; or, verb; to introduce.
Pra′ **lude** (spelled **prelude**)—a musical term; **pre**′ **lude** and **pre**′ **lude** are non-musical. All uses accent the first syllable.
Con′ **jure**—verb; to call or summon by magic.
Con jure′—(same meaning).
En′ **trance**—noun; a way for entering.
En trance′—verb; to put into a trance.
Es cort′—verb; to accompany
Es cort—noun; one who accompanies.
In′ **crease**—noun; a harvest or yield.
In crease′—verb; to grow.
In′ **val id**—noun; a disabled person.
In val′ **id**—adjective; having no force, effect, or value.
Ob′ **ject**—noun; the point of the matter.
Ob ject′—verb; to protest.
In′ **cense**—noun; perfume.
In cense′—verb; to anger.
Es′ **say**—noun; composition.
Es say′—verb; to try.

Page 16
10. PARTS OF SPEECH
Point out the nouns:
1. Horses, pasture; **2.** needle, point; **3.** clouds, summit, mountain; **4.** boys, boat, middle, stream; **5.** king, shower, distance, avenue, city; **6.** Henry, Oliver, Mr. Fields, uncle; **7.** anger, wrath.

Point out the nouns and adjectives:
Nouns—**1.** Cripple, cottage; **2.** pupils; **3.** soldier, blade; **4.** storms, isles; **5.** vessels, storm; **6.** dimes, dollars; **7.** air.

Adjectives—**1.** A, poor, that; **2.** those, studious; **3.** each, his, battle; **4.** furious, these, lovely; **5.** seven, the, late; **6.** twenty, two; **7.** the, dry, hot, still, oppressive.

Page 17
Point out the nouns, adjectives, and pronouns:
Nouns—**2.** Pencil; **3.** Home, hour; **4.** son; **5.** house, uncle's (possessive case—functions as an adjective); **6.** father, mother's, brother; **7.** farm, sale, neighborhood.
Adjectives—**2.** That; **3.** an; **5.** larger.
Pronouns—**1.** I, you; **2.** who, her; **3.** she; **4.** my (possessive case—functions as an adjective); **5.** their, our; **6.** your, her; **7.** whose; your.
Point out the nouns, pronouns, and verbs:
Nouns—**1.** Farmer, spring, fall; **2.** father, money; **3.** tears, eyes; **4.** cattle, home (**Home** may here be parsed as an adverb, or as the noun object of **to** in the elliptical prepositional phrase, **to home**); **5.** landlord; question; **7.** pupils, examination, home (noun or adverb), hearts.
Pronouns—**2.** Their, them; **3.** their; **4.** they; **5.** his; **6.** he, him; **7.** who.
Verbs—**1.** Plows; **2.** gave; **3.** sprang; **4.** followed; **5.** answered; **6.** ordered; **7.** had passed, went.

Page 18
Point out the participles:
1. Shining; **2.** picked; **3.** running; **4.** struck; **5.** folded; **6.** taken; **7.** driven.

Point out the adverbs, verbs, and adjectives:
Adverbs—**1.** Cheerfully, twice; **2.** imprudently; **3.** slowly, cautiously; **4.** never, again; **5.** not, wisely; **6.** diligently; **7.** hastily, greedily.
Verbs—**1.** Gives, gives; **2.** were managed; **3.** proceed; **4.** shall see; **5.** have acted; **6.** must study; **7.** was stolen
Adjectives—(There are no adjectives in this exercise. **Cooked**, a participle, functions as an adjective in sentence 7).

Point out the prepositions:
1. Over, into, of; **2.** from, to, in; **3.** by; **4.** up, towards, of; **5.** with, in; **6.** to, for, at.

Page 19
Point out the conjunctions and prepositions:
Conjunctions—**1.** And; **2.** or; **3.** because; **4.** neither-nor; **5.** if; **6.** but; **7.** for.
Prepositions—**2.** Upon.
Point out the interjections—(The first word in each of these sentences is an interjection).

Page 29
39. EXERCISES
Parse all the nouns:
1. Wind—noun, common, neuter, third person, singular, nominative, Rule I.
Sun (2.), **vessel** (4.), **grass** (6.), **fire** (7.), **liberty** (8.), **lead** (10.), **grammar** (12.), **fury** (13.), **health** (14.), **palace** (15.), and **defeat** (18.), are all parsed identically with **wind** in number 1.
Horses (3.), **scholars** (5.), **horse** (22.), and **friends** and **countrymen** (28.) are parsed like **wind** in number 1, except that they are common gender, sex unknown, or a mixture of both.

9. St. Helena—noun, proper, neuter, third person, singular, nominative, Rule I.
Island—noun, common, neuter, third person, singular, nominative, Rule II.
Metal (10.), **science** (12.), and **downfall** (18.), are parsed like **island**; **orator** is like **island**, except that it is masculine gender.
13. Storm's—noun, common, neuter, third person, singular, possessive, Rule III.
Henry's (14.), **King's** (15.), **Sarah's** (16.), **Boys'** (17.), and **Xerxes'** (18.) are parsed like **storms's**, except that **Henry's, Sarah's,** and **Xerxes'** are proper nouns, **Henry's, king's, boys',** and **Xerxes'** are masculine, **Sarah's** is feminine, and **boys'** is plural.
15. Fire—noun, common, third person, singular, objective case, Rule VII.
Army and **Persia** (18.), **river** (24.), **Susan** (25.), **Cincinnati** (26.), **mill** (27.), and **arms** (29.), are parsed like **fire**, with these exceptions: **Persia, Susan,** and **Cincinnati** are proper nouns; **Susan** is feminine; **arms** is plural.
16. Jane—noun, proper, feminine, third person, singular, nominative, Rule I.
Mr. Johnson (17.), **John** (19.), **Joseph** (20.), **Peter** (21.), **horse** (22.), **man** (23.), **Samuel** (24.), **Martha** (25.), **James** (26.), and **boy** (27.) are all parsed like **Jane**, with these exceptions: **horse, man,** and **boy** are common; **Mr. Johnson, John, Joseph, Peter, man, Samuel, James,** and **boy** are masculine; **horse** is common gender (**horse** is masculine when paired with **mare**; eg. Is White Lightning a horse or a mare)?
Book—noun, common, neuter, third person, singular, objective, Rule IV.
Hats (17.), **James** (19.), **book** (20.), **algebra** (21.), **boy** (22.), **letter** (23.), and **ears** is plural.
(28.) Friends, Romans, Countrymen!—nouns, common (**Romans** is proper), common gender, second person, plural, absolute case, Rule V.
Greek (29.), **daughter** (30.), **fathers** (31.), and **son** (32.) are likewise absolute case, and are parsed like **friends** . . . **Greek** is proper, common gender, singular; **daughter** is common, feminine, singular; **fathers** is common, masculine, plural; **son** is common, masculine, plural.
Friends . . . is the antecedent of **you**, the understood subject of **lend**. **Greek** is part of an ellipsis; its verb is **come**, and it is the subsequent of **they**. **Fathers** is the antecedent of **they**; and **son** is the antecedent of **him**.

Page 29-30
39. EXERCISES
Parse all the nouns:

1. Johnson—noun, proper, masculine, third person, singular, nominative, Rule I.
Shakespeare (2.), **temperance** (4.), **animals** (6.), **army** (7.), and **Platos** and **Aristotles** (8.) are parsed like **Johnson**, except that **temperance** and **animals** are neuter, **army** is common gender, and **animals, Platos,** and **Aristotles** are plural.
Doctor—noun, common, masculine gender, third person, nominative case, Rule IV.
Brother—noun, common, masculine, third person, singular, nominative, Rule II.
Johnson (second use)—noun, proper, common gender (since **Miss** or **Mrs. Johnson** might be a lawyer as well as **Mr. Johnson**), third person, singular, objective case, Rule VII.
Lawyer—noun, common, common gender, third person, singular, objective case (in apposition with **Johnson**), Rule IV.
Queen Elizabeth I's—noun, proper, feminine, third person, singular, possessive, Rule III.
Reign—noun, common, neuter, third person, singular, objective, Rule VII.
3. Warwick! Warwick!—noun, proper, masculine, second person, singular, absolute case, Rule V. (**Warwick** is the antecedent of **thou**).
4. Temperance—noun, common, neuter, third person, singular, nominative, Rule I.
Virtue—noun, common, neuter, third person, singular, nominative, Rule II.
5. King Agrippa—(parsed identical to **Warwick** in sen. 3.)
6. Classes—noun, common, neuter, third person, plural, objective. Rule VII.
Quadrupeds, fowls, fishes, reptiles, and **insects**—nouns, common, neuter, third person, plural, absolute case, Rule V.
7. Day—noun, common, neuter, third person, singular, objective, Rule VII.
8. Platos and **Aristotles**—nouns, proper, masculine, third person, plural, nominative, Rule I.
9. Mr. Squires—noun, proper, masculine, third person, singular, objective, Rule VI.
Bookseller and **stationer**—nouns, common, masculine, third person, singular, objective, Rule IV.

Correct all errors:
1. Brothers-in-law; **2.** Knights Templar; **3.** nebulae (**nebulas** is acceptable; **nebulae** is preferred); **4.** Mrs. Johnsons; **5.** Steele the banker's; **6.** Jones; **7.** boy's (or **boys'**, if the slate belonged to more than one boy); **8.** Men's; **9.** sister Susan's; **10.** O. B. Pierce's; **11.** octavos, quartos, and **folios**; **12.** chimneys; **13.** phenomena.

Page 32
THE ADJECTIVE
Tell which of the adjectives in the following sentences are descriptive, and which are compound and participial:

1. **Unfortunate**—des.; **hard—working**—comp., consisting of **hard**, des., and **working**, part.
2. **Beautiful**—des.
3. **English**—des.; **costly**—des.
4. **Howling**—part.; **past**—des. (**Passed** is a misprint).
5. **Productive**—des.
6. **Marble**—des.
7. **New England** and **Australian** are descriptive.

Page 39
55. EXERCISES
Parse the nouns and adjectives:

Nouns—**Report, storms, life, walks, fields, road, soldier, horses, law, story, fields, floor, storms, company, war, shade, urn, bust, current,** and **eyes**—all nouns, common, neuter gender (except **soldier**, masculine, and **horses**, common gender), third person, singular or plural as shown by form, nominative case, Rule I.

2. **Islands**—noun, common, neuter, third person, plural, objective, Rule VII.
3. **Vapor**—noun, common, neuter, third person, singular, nominative, Rule II.
7. **View**—noun, common, neuter, third person, singular, objective, Rule VI.
Subject—noun, common, neuter, third person, singular, objective, Rule VII.
8. **Town**—(parsed identical to **subject**).
11. **Disgrace**—(parsed identical to **vapor**).

State, concert (12.), boards (16.), concerns, election (18.), years, session (both uses), circle (circle is the object of **round and round), arguments... expedients (20.), mist, years, power (21.), mansion (22.), course, joy (23.), rapture, day (24.), step ... groan,** and **hill (25.),** are all nouns, objects of their respective prepositions; common, neuter gender, third person, singular (except that **boards, concerns, years, arguments, expedients,** and **years** are plural), objective case, Rule VII.

12. **Lines**—noun, common, neuter, third person, plural, objective, Rule VI.
13. **Powers**—noun, common, neuter, second person, plural, absolute case, Rule V.
17. **Great** (both uses)—nouns, common, common gender, third person, plural, nominative case, Rule I. (Number 17 is an elliptical sentence which in full reads, **None think (that) the great (are) unhappy but the great, (who think themselves unhappy)**.

18. **Story**—noun, common, neuter, third person, singular, objective (**story** is the object of **to make**), Rule VI.
19. **Front**—noun, common, neuter, third person, singular, objective, Rule VI.
22. **Breath**—noun, common, neuter, third person, singular, objective (object of **can call**), Rule VI.
24. **Dawn**—noun, common, neuter, third person, singular, objective (object of **see**), Rule VI.
25. **Stone**—noun, common, neuter, third person, singular, objective (object of **heaves**), Rule VI.

Adjectives—
1. **A** (also in **7, 9, 18,** and **25**)—adjective, definitive, indefinite article, it cannot be compared; belongs to **report, view, host, story,** or **stone**, Rule XII.
Loud—adjective, descriptive (**loud, louder, loudest**), positive, belongs to **report**, Rule XII.
2. **Fearful**—adjective, descriptive (**fearful, more fearful, most fearful**), positive degree, belongs to **storms**, Rule XII.
These (also in **4**)—adjective, demonstrative, plural of **this**, it cannot be compared; belongs to **islands** or **walks**, Rule XII.
Beautiful—adjective, descriptive (**beautiful, more beautiful, most beautiful**), positive, belongs to **islands**, Rule XII.
3. **But a**—adjective, indefinite, cannot be compared; belongs to **vapor**, Rule XII. (Some authorities consider **but** here to be an adverb. This makes no grammatical sense, since **vapor**, a noun, must be modified by an adjective.)
4. **Quiet, secluded**—adjectives, descriptive (**quiet, quieter, quietest; secluded, more secluded, most secluded**), positive degree, belongs to **walks**, Rule XII.
5. **Sad, lonely**—adjectives, descriptive (**sad, sadder, saddest; lonely, lonelier, loneliest**), positive, belongs to I, Rule XII.
6. **Green**—adjective, descriptive, (**green, greener, greenest**), positive, belongs to **fields**, Rule XII.
7. **Twofold**—adjective, numeral multiplicative, it cannot be compared; belongs to **view**, Rule XII.
The (also in **12, 15, 16, 17**-twice, **18**-thrice, **21**-twice, **22, 23, 24,** and **25**)—adjective, definitive, definite article, it cannot be compared; belongs to **subject, lines, fields, floor, great** (both uses), **company, concerns, election, mist, shade, breath, current, dawn,** or **hill**, Rule XII.
8. **Either**—adjective, definitive, distributive, pronominal, it cannot be compared; belongs to **road**, Rule XII.
9. **Each**—adjective, definitive, distributive pro-

nominal, it cannot be compared; belongs to **soldier**, Rule XII.

10. Both—adjective, definitive, demonstrative pronominal, it cannot be compared; belongs to **horses**, Rule XII.

Lame—adjective, descriptive (**lame, lamer lamest**), positive, belongs to **horses**, Rule XII.

11. Such a—adjective, indefinitive, it cannot be compared; belongs to **law**, Rule XII.

Any—adjective, definitive, indefinite pronominal, it cannot be compared; belongs to **state**, Rule XII.

12. First—adjective, definitive, numeral, ordinal, it cannot be compared; belongs to **lines**, Rule XII.

Four—Adjective, definitive, numeral, cardinal, it cannot be compared; belongs to **lines, Rule XII.**

13. Drowsy—adjective, descriptive (**drowsy, drowsier, drowsiest**), positive, belongs to **powers**, Rule XII.

14. One—adjective, definitive, numeral, cardinal, it cannot be compared; belongs to **story**, Rule XII.

Good—adjective, descriptive (good, better, best), positive, belongs to **story**, Rule XII.

(**Told**, past participle of **tell**, is the verb of **another**. It makes no difference to the sense of the sentence whether it is parsed as an adjective modifying **another**—as in **a well-told story**—or as a verb. Convention, however, requires that it be parsed as a verb).

15. Australian—adjective, descriptive, it cannot be compared; belongs to **fields**, Rule XII.

Gold—adjective, descriptive, it cannot be compared; belongs to **fields**, Rule XII.

Extensive—adjective, descriptive (**extensive, more extensive, most extensive**), positive, belongs to **fields**, Rule XII.

16. Six-inch—adjective, descriptive; compound of **six**, a cardinal numeral, and **inch**, a noun; it cannot be compared; belongs to **boards**, Rule XII.

17. Unhappy—adjective, descriptive (**unhappy, unhappier, unhappiest**), positive, belongs to **great**, Rule XII.

18. Long, short—adjectives, descriptive (**long, longer, longest; short, shorter, shortest**), positive, belongs to **story**, Rule XII.

More important—adjective, descriptive (**important, more important, most important**), comparative, belongs to **concerns**, Rule XII.

19. Grim-visaged—compound adjective, descriptive (**grim-visaged, grimmer-visaged, grimmest-visaged**), positive, belongs to **war**, Rule XII.

Wrinkled—adjective, descriptive (**wrinkled, more wrinkled, most wrinkled**), positive, belongs to **front**, Rule XII.

20. Nine—adjective, definitive, numeral, cardinal, it cannot be compared; belongs to **years**, Rule XII.

Long—adjective, descriptive (**long, longer, longest**), positive, belongs to **years**, Rule XII.

This—(and in 24)—adjective, demonstrative pronominal, it cannot be compared; belongs to **circle** (20.) and **day** (24.), Rule XII.

Miserable—(both uses)—adjective, descriptive (**miserable, more miserable, most miserable**), positive, belongs to **circle** and **expedients**, Rule XII.

Occasional—adjective, descriptive, cannot be compared; belongs to **arguments**, Rule XII.

21. Dim—adjective, descriptive (**dim, dimmer, dimmest**), positive, belongs to **shade**, Rule XII.

(**Gray**, ordinarily an adjective, is here used by Byron instead of the adverb **grayly** to fit this iambic measure. It modifies **flits**, the verb of the subject, **shade**. This is **poetic license**.)

22. Storied, animated, fleeting—adjectives, descriptive, they cannot be compared; belong to **urn, bust,** or **breath**, Rule XII.

23. Secret, loud, smooth—adjectives, descriptive (**secret, more secret, most secret; loud, louder, loudest; smooth, smoother, smoothest**), positive belong to **course, storms,** or **current**, Rule XII.

No—adjective, definitive, indefinite pronominal, it cannot be compared; belongs to **storms**, Rule XII.

Domestic—adjective, descriptive, it cannot be compared; belongs to **joy**, Rule XII.

24. Opening, returning—adjectives, descriptive, they cannot be compared; belong to **eyes** or **day**, Rule XII.

25. Many a (both uses)—adjective, definitive, indefinite pronominal, it cannot be compared; belongs to **step** and **groan**, Rule XII.

Weary, high—adjectives, descriptive (**weary, wearier, weariest; high, higher, highest**—or **most high**—emphatic), positive, belong to **step** or **hill**, Rule XII.

Huge—adjective, descriptive (**huge, huger, hugest**), positive, belongs to **stone**, Rule XII.

Round—adjective, descriptive (**round** is not ordinarily compared, since it refers to a perfect circle; however, in reference to stones, etc., which are usually imperfectly round, it may be compared: **round, rounder, roundest**), positive, belongs to **stone**, Rule XII.

Page 46
THE PRONOUN
65. EXERCISES

Parse the nouns, personal pronouns, and adjectives:

Nouns—**School** (1.), **sister** (2.), **book** (2. and 7.), **feet**, and **way** (12.)—nouns, common neuter (**sister** is feminine), third person, singular (**feet** is plural), objective case (direct or indirect objects of the verbs **attend, gave, bought,** and **teach**), Rule VI.

Eyes (4.), **work, hands** (6), **house** (8.), **way** (9.), **number, some** (10.), and **liberty** (11.) are nouns, common, neuter, third person, singular (**eyes** and **hands** are plural), objective (objects of the pronouns **with, in, of, in, on, of, with,** or **of**), Rule VII.

6. **Wicked**—noun, common, common gender, third person, singular, nominative, Rule I.

11. **Country, land**—nouns, common, common gender, second person, singular, absolute case, Rule V.

12. **Instructor**—noun, proper, masculine (noun and pronoun appellations for deity, in the original Hebrew and Greek scriptures, as well as the English Bible, are consistently of the masculine gender: eg., **Father, Lord, He Who Is**), second person, singular, absolute case, Rule V.

Adjectives—1. **Same**—adjective, definitive, demonstrative pronominal, it cannot be compared; belongs to **school**, Rule XII.

2. **New**—adjective, descriptive (**new, newer, newest**), positive, belongs to **book**, Rule XII.

4. **Own** (also in 6.)—adjective, definitive, indefinite pronominal, it cannot be compared; belongs to **eyes** or **hands**, Rule XII.

6. **The** (also in 7. and 10.)—adjective, definitive, definite article, it cannot be compared; belongs to **wicked, book,** or **number**, Rule XII.

10. **Wise**—adjective, descriptive (**wise, wiser, wisest**), positive, belongs to **they**, Rule XII.

11. **Sweet**—adjective, descriptive (**sweet, sweeter, sweetest**), positive, belongs to **land**, Rule XII.

12. **Great**—adjective, descriptive (**great, greater, greatest**), positive, belongs to **Instructor**, Rule XII.

Erring—adjective, descriptive, it cannot be compared; belongs to **feet**, Rule XII.

Personal pronouns—1. **He**—pronoun, personal, simple, its antecedent is the name, understood, of the person spoken of; masculine gender, third person, singular to agree with its antecedent, Rule IX; nominative case, Rule I.

I—pronoun, personal, simple, its antecedent is the name, understood, of the person speaking; gender, first person, singular to agree with its antecedent, Rule IX; nominative, Rule I.

2. **She**—pronoun, personal, simple, its antecedent is the name, understood, of the person spoken of; feminine gender, third person, singular to agree with its antecedent, Rule IX; nominative case, Rule I.

Her—pronoun, personal, simple, its antecedent is the name, understood, of the person spoken of; feminine gender, third person, singular to agree with its antecedent, Rule IX; possessive case, Rule III.

3. **You**—pronoun, personal, simple, its antecedent is the name, understood, of the person spoken to; unknown gender, second person, unknown number to agree with its antecedent, Rule IX; nominative case, Rule I.

Him—pronoun, personal, simple, its antecedent is the name, understood, of the person spoken of; masculine gender, third person, singular to agree with its antecedent, Rule IX; objective case, Rule VI.

4. **I** (also in numbers 7, 9, 11, and 12)—these are parsed identically to **I** in number 1.

It—pronoun, personal, simple, its antecedent is the name, understood, of the thing spoken of; neuter gender, third person, singular to agree with its antecedent, Rule IX; objective case, Rule VI.

My—pronoun, personal, simple, its antecedent is the name, understood, of the person speaking; unknown gender, first person, singular to agree with its antecedent, Rule IX; possessive case, Rule III.

5. **You**—pronoun, personal, simple, its antecedent is the name, understood, of the person spoken to; unknown gender, second person, singular to agree with its antecedent, Rule IX; nominative case, Rule I.

Yourself—pronoun, compound personal, its antecedent is the name, understood, of the person spoken to; unknown gender, second person, singular to agree with its antecedent, Rule IX; nominative case, in apposition with **you**, Rule IV.

Me—pronoun, personal, simple, its antecedent is the name, understood, of the speaker; unknown gender, first person, singular to agree with its antecedent, Rule IX; objective case, Rule VI.

6. **His**—pronoun, personal, simple, its antecedent is the name, understood, of the person spoken of; masculine, third person, singular to agree with its antecedent, Rule IX; possessive case, Rule III.

7. **It**—(parsed identical with **it** in 4.)

8. **They**—pronoun, personal, simple, its antecedent is the name, understood, of the persons spoken of; common gender, third person, plural to agree with its antecedent, Rule IX; nominative case, Rule I.

Our—pronoun, personal, simple, its antecedent is the name, understood, of the persons speaking; common gender, first person, plural to agree with its antecedent, Rule IX; possessive case, Rule III.

9. **Their**—pronoun, personal, simple, its antecedent is the name understood, of the persons spoken

of; common gender, third person, plural to agree with its antecedent, Rule IX; possessive case, Rule III.

10. We—pronoun, personal, simple, its antecedent is the name, understood, of the persons speaking; common gender, first person, plural to agree with its antecedent, Rule IX; nominative case, Rule I.

Ourselves (both uses)—pronoun, compound personal, its antecedent is the name, understood, of the speakers; common gender, first person, plural to agree with its antecedent, Rule IX; objective case, Rule VI.

Themselves (first, second, and fourth usages)—pronoun, compound personal, its antecedent is the name, understood, of the persons spoken of; common gender, third person, plural to agree with its antecedent, Rule IX; objective case (object of the verbs **commend**, **measuring**, or **comparing**), Rule VI.

Themselves (third and fifth usages)—pronoun, compound personal, its antecedent is the name, understood, of the persons spoken of; common gender, third person, plural to agree with its antecedent, Rule IX; objective case (object of the prepositions **by** or **among**), Rule VII.

11. My—pronoun, personal, simple, its antecedent is the name, understood, of the speaker(s)/singer(s); common gender, first person, plural to agree with its antecedent, Rule IX; possessive case, Rule III.

It (subject of **is** in the contraction 'tis) pronoun, personal, simple, **it** has no antecedent (the use here is idiomatic, as in **it is raining**); neuter gender, third person, singular, to agree with conventional use, Rule IX; nominative case, Rule I.

Thee (both uses)—pronoun, personal, simple, its antecedent is **country**; neuter, second person, singular, to agree with country, Rule IX; objective case, Rule VII.

12. Thou (first usage)—pronoun, personal, simple, its subsequent is **Instructor**, to which it is in apposition; masculine case, second person singular to agree with **Instructor**, Rule IX; absolute case, Rule IV.

Thou (second usage)—pronoun, personal, simple, its antecedent **Instructor**; masculine, second person, singular to agree with **Instructor**, Rule IX; nominative case, Rule I.

My—pronoun, personal simple, its antecedent is the name, understood, of the speaker; unknown gender, first person, singular to agree with its antecedent, Rule IX; possessive case, Rule III.

Thy—pronoun, personal, simple, its antecedent is **Instructor**; masculine, second person, singular to agree with **Instructor**, Rule IX; possessive case, Rule III.

Page 47
66-69. POSSESSIVE PRONOUNS/EXERCISES
Parse the possessive pronouns:

1. His—pronoun, possessive, it represents both the possessor and the thing possessed; its antecedent is **farm**; neuter, third person, singular to agree with its antecedent, Rule IX; nominative case, it is used as the predicate of the proposition, **The farm is . . . his**, Rule II.

Theirs—parsed similar to **his**; equivalent to **their own**. Theirs is plural, since the possessor is plural.

2. Yours—pronoun, possessive, its antecedent is **horse**; common gender, third person, singular to agree with its antecedent, Rule IX; objective, it is the object of the preposition **of**, Rule VII.

3. Yours—parsed like **yours** in sentence 2, except that its antecedent is **lecture**.

4. Ours—pronoun, possessive, its antecedent is **friend**; equivalent to **our friend**, common gender, third person, plural, to agree with its antecedent, Rule IX; objective, Rule VII. (The possessor is plural; the thing possessed is singular—**ours** represents both).

5. Mine—pronoun, possessive, its antecedent is **book**; neuter, third person, singular to agree with its antecedent, Rule IX; nominative, Rule II.

His/hers—pronouns, possessive, their antecedent is **it**, which in turn has **book** for its antecedent; equivalent to **his** or **her book**, neuter gender, third person, singular to agree with its antecedent, Rule IX; nominative case, Rule II.

6. Theirs—pronoun, possessive, its antecedent is **carriage**; neuter, third person, plural to agree with its antecedent, Rule IX; objective case, Rule VII.

7. Mine—pronoun, possessive, its antecedent is **friend**; common gender, second person, singular to agree with its antecedent, Rule IX; objective, Rule VII.

Page 51
74. EXERCISES
Parse the relative pronouns:

1. Who—pronoun, relative, simple, its antecedent is **those**; common gender, third person, plural, Rule IX; nominative, Rule I.

2. That—pronoun, relative, simple, its antecedent is **he**; common gender (**he** is here either male or female), third person, singular to agree with its antecedent, Rule IX; nominative, it is the subject of the subordinaate clause, **that hateth**, Rule I.

3. That—pronoun, relative, simple, its antecedent is **they**; common gender, third person, plural to agree with its antecedent, Rule IX; nominative, it is the subject of the subordinate clause, **that forsake the law**, Rule I.

As—pronoun, relative, simple, its antecedent is **such**; common gender, third person, plural to agree with its antecedent, Rule IX; nominative (**as** is the subject of the adjective clause, **as keep the law**, modifying **such**. **Such content with them** is the second coordinating clause in this compound sentence), Rule I.

4. **That**—pronoun, relative, simple, its antecedent is **persons**; common gender, third person, plural to agree with its antecedent, Rule IX; objective case, it is the object of **dislike**, Rule VI.

Who—pronoun, relative, simple, its antecedent is **those**, which has **persons** as its antecedent; common gender, third person, plural to agree with its antecedent, Rule IX; nominative, Rule I.

5. **Which**—pronoun, relative, simple, its antecedent is **house**; neuter, third person, singular to agree with its antecedent, Rule IX; objective, it is the object of **admire**, Rule VI.

Whom—pronoun, relative, simple, its antecedent is **man**; masculine, third person, singular to agree with its antecedent, Rule IX; objective, it is the object of **see**, Rule VI.

6. **Whatever**—pronoun, relative, compound, equivalent to **that which**. Parse **that** as a demonstrative pronominal adjective (cf. text, p. 33) used as a noun, the subject of **is right**. **Which** is the relative, subject of **is**, first usage; its antecedent is **that**; simple, neuter, third person, singular to agree with its antecedent, Rule IX; nominative, Rule I.

7. **Whatsoever**—pronoun, relative, compound, it has no antecedent; neuter, third person, singular; objective, it is the object of **shall ask**, Rule VI.

That—pronoun, relative, simple, its antecedent is the clause, **Whatsoever ye shall ask in my name**; neuter, third person, singular to agree with its antecedent, Rule IX; objective, it is the object of **will do**, Rule VI.

8. **What**—pronoun, relative, it is a double relative equivalent to **that which**. Parse **that** as a pronominal adjective used as a noun, the object of **will do**. **Which** is a pronoun, relative, simple, its antecedent is **that**; neuter, third person, singular to agree with its antecedent, Rule IX; nominative case, subject of **is**, Rule I.

9. **That** (first four uses)—pronouns, relative, simple, its antecedent is **dog, cat, rat,** or **malt**; common gender (**dog, cat, rat**; neuter—**malt**), third person, singular to agree with its antecedents, Rule IX; nominative case, subject of **worried, killed, ate,** or **lay**, Rule I.

That (fifth use)—pronoun, relative, simple, its antecedent is house; neuter, third person, singular to agree with its antecedent, Rule IX; objective, object of **built**, Rule VI.

10. **Whatever**—pronoun, relative, compound, equivalent to **that which**. Parse **that** as a pronominal adjective used as a noun, the object of **doing**. **Which** is a pronoun, relative, simple, its antecedent is **that**; neuter, third person, singular to agree with its antecedent, Rule IX; nominative case, subject of **injures**, Rule I.

Page 52
78. INTERROGATIVE PRONOUNS
Parse the interrogative pronouns:

1. **Who**—pronoun, interrogative, it asks a question; indefinite gender and number indeterminate, third person; nominative case, Rule I.

2. **Whose**—pronoun, interrogative, indefinite subsequent, gender and number indeterminate, third person, possessive case, modifies **house**, Rule III.

3. **Whom**—pronoun, interrogative, subsequent is **James**; masculine, third person, singular to agree with its subsequent, Rule IX; objective, object of **did call**, Rule VI.

4. **Whom**—pronoun, interrogative, subsequent is indefinite; gender and number indeterminate, third person; objective, Rule VII.

5. **Which**—pronoun, interrogative, subsequent is **book**; neuter, third person, singular to agree with its subsequent; objective, object of **will have**, Rule VI.

6. **Whom**—pronoun, interrogative, subsequent is **me**; gender indeterminate, first person singular to agree with its subsequent; objective, object of **to be**, Rule VI.

7. **What**—pronoun, interrogative, subsequent is **wait**; neuter, third person, singular to agree with its subsequent, Rule IX; objective, Rule VI.

8. **What**—pronoun, interrogative, subsequent is indefinite, neuter, third person, singular; nominative case, Rule I.

9. **Which**—pronoun, interrogative, subsequent is **lesson**; neuter, third person, singular to agree with its subsequent, Rule IX, nominative, Rule I.

10. **Who**—pronoun, interrogative, subsequent is indefinite; gender indeterminate, third person, singular; nominative, Rule I.

Parse the relative and interrogative pronouns:
1. **Who**—pronoun, interrogative, subsequent is **father**; masculine, third person, singular to agree with its subsequent, Rule IX; nominative, Rule I.

2. **Who**—pronoun, relative, simple, antecedent is indefinite; gender and number indeterminate, third person; nominative, Rule I.

3. **What**—pronoun, relative, simple, equivalent to **that which**. Parse **that** as a pronominal adjective used as a noun, direct object of **tell** (**me** is **tell's** indirect object). **Which**—pronoun, relative, simple, its antecedent is **that**; neuter, third person, singular to agree with its antecedent, Rule IX; objective case, object of **should do**, Rule VI.

4. **What**—(**What** is here a pronominal adjective modifying **vessel**; **that** is likewise a pronominal adjective in this elliptical sentence, **What vessel is that (vessel)**. The sentence has no interrogatives nor relatives).

5. **What**—pronoun, double relative, equivalent to **that which**, **that** being the antecedent and **which**, the relative. Parse **that** as a pronominal adjective used as a noun, object of the preposition **for**.

Which—pronoun, relative, its antecedent is **that**; neuter, third person, singular, objective case, object of **need**, Rule VI.

6. **Whose**—pronoun, interrogative, its subsequent is **Mr. Hubbard**; masculine, third person, singular to agree with its subsequent, Rule IX; possessive case, Rule III.

(Some grammarians treat **whose** in this construction as a pronominal adjective, like **what** in sentence 4; most others concur with **Harvey**, and this seems most consistent with the word's etymology, though the sentence construction does allow either treatment. Webster admits **whose** as a possessive pronoun only).

7. **Which**—conjunctive pronoun, relative, its antecedent is the clause, **the boy closed the shutters**; simple, neuter, third person, singular, Rule IX; nominative case, subject of **darkened**, Rule I.

Note—*Sentence 7 is a grammatical construction which some grammarians insist should be avoided, yet the use of **which** to refer to an entire clause has ample precedent in literate English.* **Webster's International Dictionary** *offers this explanation:* **Which** *is "A relative pronoun, used especially in referring to an antecedent noun or clause, but sometimes with reference to what is specified or implied in a sentence . . . ."* **Webster** *then illustrates with Shakespeare:*

> "And when thou fail'st—as
> God forbid the hour!—
> Must Edward fall, **which** peril
> heaven forfend!"

Which's antecedent is here the clause, **Edward must fall**.

8. **What**—pronoun, interrogative, its subsequent is **name**; masculine, third person, singular, Rule IX; nominative, Rule II.

9. **Whoever**—pronoun, relative, compound, it is equivalent to **he who**, **he** being the antecedent part and **who** the relative. Parse **he** as a personal pronoun, subject of **should have**, and **who** as a relative.

Who—pronoun, relative, its antecedent is **he**, simple masculine, third person, singular, Rule IX; nominative case, subject of **enters**, Rule I. (For diagramming, rewrite this sentence, **He should have a pure heart who enters here**.

10. **That**—pronoun, relative, its antecedent is **all**; simple, neuter, third person, singular, Rule IX; objective, it is the object of **had**, Rule VI.

Pages 52-53

Parse the nouns, pronouns, and adjectives

Nouns—**Virtue** (1.), **garment** (3.), **ounce** (4.), **prayers** (5.), **man** (6.), **army** (7.), **liberty** (12.), **death** (13.), **heart** (14.), **cares** (15.); and **glad**, **brood**, and **one** (18.)—nouns common, neuter (**man**—masculine), third person, singular (**prayers**, **cares**, and **glad** (substitute for **ones**—plural), nominative, the subjects of **is**, **is**, **made**, **is**, **are ended**, **went**, **is**, **was**, **is**, **is**, **beseige**, **will laugh**, **plod** or **will chase**, Rule I.

Condition (1.), **light** (2.), **ounces** (4.), and **bondman** (10.)—nouns, common, neuter (**bondman**—masculine), third person, singular (**ounces**—plural), nominative, Rule II.

Happiness (1.), **world** (2.), **gold, silver** (4.), **David, Jesse** (5.), **house** (6.), **spoils, nations** (7.), **mind** (8.), **world** (9.), **men** (11.), **men** (12.) **Socrates, friends** (13.) **man, charms** (14.), **fancy, fate** (15.), **trust, dust** (16.), **heart, eye, bosom, sky** (17.), and **care** (18.,—nouns, common (**David, Jesse**, and **Socrates**—proper), neuter (**David, Jesse, men, men, Socrates,** and **man**—masculine; **friends**—common gender), third person, singular (**spoils, nations, friends,** and **charms**—plural), objective case; they are used as the objects of the prepositions **of, of, of, of, of, of, to, with, of, of, in, to, as, of, with, of, against, from, from, to, in, of, with, along,** or **of**; Rule VII.

5. **Son**—noun, common, masculine, third person, singular, objective, in apposition with **David**, Rule IV.

State, strokes (15.), **treasure, relics, room** (16.), **spirit, steps, storm** (17.), **phantom, mirth, employment,** and **bed** (18.)—nouns, common, neuter, third person, singular (**strokes, relics,** and **steps**—plural), objective case; they are used as the objects of the verbs **beseige, feel, unveil, take, give, let share, follow, heed, will chase, shall leave,** or **shall make,** Rule VI.

12. **Men** (second usage)—noun, common, masculine, third person, plural, objective; **men** is the complement of **themselves**, object of **did esteem**.

It is the same case, Rule IV.

Applause (14.), **tomb** (16.), and **independence** (17.)—nouns of direct address by personification, common, feminine (**tomb** and **independence**—gender unknown), second person, singular, absolute case, Rule V.

14. Proof—noun, common, neuter, third person, singular, nominative case, Rule II.

Pronouns—2. **Ye**—pronoun, personal, simple, its antecedents are the names, understood, of the persons spoken to; common gender first person, plural (Elizabethan plural of **thou** or **you**), Rule IX; nominative, Rule I.

6. His own—pronoun, possessive, its subsequent is **house**; neuter, third person, singular, objective, Rule VII.

8. One another (Here see pages 35-36, "General Remarks." **One another** may be parsed as a pronoun or as "adjectives used as nouns"; in either case, the result is the same). It is a pronoun, common, common gender, second person, plural, objective, object of the preposition **toward**, Rule VII.

9. He (both uses)—pronoun, personal, simple, its antecedent is the name, understood, of the person spoken of; masculine, third person, singular, Rule IX; nominative, Rule I.

Everything (**Everything** may be parsed as an indefinite pronominal adjective used as a noun, or as an indefinite pronoun. Grammarians differ. It functions here as a relative pronoun to introduce the noun clause **everything he had in the world**. The clause is the direct object of the verb **sacrificed**.) **Everything** is in the objective case, third person, singular, neuter gender; Rule VI.

What—pronoun, interrogative, its subsequent is indefinite, neuter, third person, singular, Rule IX; objective case, it is the object of **could ask**, Rule VI.

We—pronoun, simple, its antecedents are the names understood, of the persons speaking; common gender, first person, plural, Rule IX; nominative case, Rule I.

10. Who—pronoun, interrogative, its subsequent is **bondman**; masculine, second person, singular, Rule IX; nominative, Rule I.

11. I (both uses)—pronoun, personal, simple, its antecedent is the name of the person speaking; gender unknown, first person, singular, Rule IX; nominative, Rule I.

Ye—pronoun, personal, simple, its antecedent is **men**; common gender, second person, plural, Rule IX; nominative, the subject of the verb **judge**, Rule I. (In this quote from I Corinthians 10:15, as in all quotations from the King James Bible and Elizabethan sources, **ye** is the nominative plural of **thou**. In the eighteenth and nineteenth centuries, however, **ye** became a colloquialized form of **you**, either singular or plural, while **thou** and **thee** disappeared. Today **ye** is rarely heard except in provincial dialect, singular or plural. **Men** is here generic; either sex is meant).

What—pronoun, double relative, equivalent to **that which**, **that** being the antecedent part, and **which**, the relative. Parse **that** as a pronominal adjective used as a noun, in the objective case after **judge**.

Which—pronoun, relative, its antecedent is **that**; neuter, third person, singular, objective, object of **say**, Rule VI.

12. Theirs—pronoun, possessive, it represents both the possessor and the thing possessed; its antecedent is **liberty**; neuter, third person, plural, Rule IX; nominative, Rule II. (**Theirs** is plural of **they**, which is an apparent contradiction of Rule IX, since the stated antecedent, **liberty**, is singular. But **Theirs** represents the possessor, **men**, as well, and it is from the possessor that possessive pronouns take their number).

It—pronoun, personal, simple, its antecedent is **liberty**; neuter, third person, singular, Rule IX; objective, Rule VII.

They—pronoun, personal, simple, its antecedent is **men**; common gender, third person, plural, Rule IX; nominative, Rule I.

Themselves—pronoun, personal, compound, its antecedent is **men**; common gender, third person, plural, Rule IX; objective, Rule VI.

13. His—pronoun, personal, simple, its antecedent is **Socrates**; masculine, third person, singular, Rule IX; possessive case, Rule III.

That—pronoun, relative, its antecedent is **death**; simple, neuter, third person, singular, Rule IX; nominative, it is the subject of **could be desired**, Rule I.

14. Thy—pronoun, personal, simple, its antecedent is **applause**; feminine (because of personification), second person, singular, Rule IX; possessive case, Rule III.

15. Our—pronoun, personal, simple, its antecedents are the names, understood, of the speakers; common gender, first person, plural, Rule IX; possessive, Rule III.

We—pronoun, personal, simple, its antecedents are the names, understood, of the speakers; common gender, first person, plural, Rule IX; nominative case, Rule I.

16. Thy (both uses)—pronouns, parsed identically to **thy** in **14**, except that its subsequent is **tomb**.

17. Thy (both uses)—pronoun, parsed identically to **thy** in **14** and **16**, except that its subsequent is **Independence . . . Lord**, masculine.

PAGE 53-59

I (In contraction as **I'll**, and also as the understood subject of **heed**)—pronouns, personal, simple, its antecedent is the name, understood, of the speaker; gender unknown, first person, singular, Rule IX; nominative, Rule I.

18. Thou/thee—pronouns, personal, simple, their antecedent is the name, understood, of the person spoken to/reader; unknown gender, second person, singular, Rule IX; nominative, Rule I (**thou**)/objective, Rule VII (**thee**).

One—pronoun, indefinite, simple, its antecedent is the name, understood, of the person spoken of; common gender, third person, singular, Rule IX; nominative, Rule I.

His—pronoun, personal, simple, its antecedent is the understood name of the person spoken of; common gender, third person, singular, Rule IX; possessive case, Rule III.

These—pronoun, demonstrative, its antecedents are the names, understood, of the persons spoken of; common gender, third person, plural, Rule IX; nominative, Rule I.

Their (All three uses)—pronoun, personal, simple, its antecedents are the names, understood, of the persons spoken of; common gender, third person, plural, Rule IX; possessive case, Rule III.

Adjectives—**The** (in **1, 2, 5, 7, 8, 9, 13, 16, 17,** and **18**)—adjectives, definitive, definite article, it cannot be compared; belongs to **condition, light, world, son, spoils, mind, world, death, (the most pleasant death), dust, heart, eye, storm,** or **glad**; Rule XII.

3. That—adjective, definitive, demonstrative pronominal; it cannot be compared; belongs to **garment**, Rule XII.

4. One, sixteen—adjectives, definitives, numerals, cardinals, they cannot be compared; belong to **ounce** or **ounces**, Rule XII.

6. Every—adjective, definitive, distributive pronominal, it cannot be compared; belongs to **man**, Rule XII.

7. Many—adjective, definitive, indefinite pronominal (**many, more, most**), positive, belongs to **nations**, Rule XII.

8. Same—adjective, demonstrative pronominal, it cannot be compared; belongs to **mind**, Rule XII.

9. More—adjective, definitive, indefinite pronominal (**much, more, most**), comparative, belongs to **what**, Rule XII.

10. Base—adjective, descriptive (**base, baser, basest**), positive, belongs to **who**, Rule XII.

11. Wise—adjective, descriptive, (**wise, wiser, wisest**), positive, belongs to **men**, Rule XII.

13. Most pleasant—adjective, descriptive, (**pleasant, more pleasant, most pleasant**), superlative, belongs to **death**, Rule XII.

14. Popular—adjective, descriptive, (**popular, more popular, most popular**), positive, belongs to **applause**, Rule XII.

What (also in **15**)—adjective, definitive, indefinite pronominal, it cannot be compared; belongs to **heart, cares,** or **strokes** (doubled for emphasis before **cares**—**what, what black, ceaseless cares**), Rule XII.

Sweet—adjective, descriptive (**sweet, sweeter, sweetest**), positive, belongs to **charms**, Rule XII.

Seducing—adjective, descriptive, (**seducing, more seducing, most seducing**), positive, belongs to **charms**, Rule XII.

15. Ceaseless—adjective, descriptive, it cannot be compared; belongs to **cares**, Rule XII.

16. Faithful—adjective, descriptive (**faithful, more faithful, most faithful**), positive, belongs to **tomb**, Rule XII.

New—adjective, descriptive (**new, newer, newest**), positive, belongs to **treasure**, Rule XII.

Sacred—adjective, descriptive, (**sacred, more sacred, most sacred**), positive, belongs to **relics**, Rule XII.

Silent—adjective, descriptive (**silent, more silent, most silent**), positive belongs to **dust**, Rule XII.

17. Lion—adjective, descriptive, it cannot be compared; belongs to **heart**, Rule XII.

Eagle—adjective, descriptive, it cannot be compared; belongs to **eye**, Rule XII.

18. Solemn—adjective, descriptive (**solemn, solemner, solemnest/solemn, more solemn, most solemn**), positive, belongs to **brood**, Rule XII.

Favorite—adjective, descriptive (**favorite, more favorite, most favorite**), positive, belongs to **phantom**, Rule XII.

Page 58
86. EXERCISES
Tell which of the verbs . . . are active/passive:
1. Active; **2.** passive (**The news astonished John**—active); 3. active; 4. passive; 5. active; 6. passive; 7. active; 8. active; 9. active.

Page 59
88. EXERCISES
Give the present, perfect, and compound participles:

relying	relied	having relied
finding	found	having found
helping	helped	having helped
studying	studied	having studied
reciting	recited	having recited

inquiring	inquired	having inquired
answering	answered	having answered
plowing	plowed	having plowed
cultivating	cultivated	having cultivated
joining	joined	having joined
emulating	emulated	having emulated
spelling	spelled	having spelled
growing	grown	having grown
painting	painted	having painted
resembling	resembled	having resembled
hoping	hoped	having hoped
suffering	suffered	having suffered
sitting	sat	having sat
seeing	saw	having seen
going	went	having gone
coming	came	having come
laying	laid	having laid
arriving	arrived	having arrived
exhausting	exhausted	having exhausted
enjoying	enjoyed	having enjoyed
writing	wrote	having written
reading	read	having read
ventilating	ventilated	having ventilated

Page 61

Parse the nouns, pronouns, adjectives, and participles:

Nouns—Bells (1.), **letter** (2.), **sails** (5.), **farm** (6.), **men** (8.), **ripple** and **water** (13.), and **repose** (14.)—nouns, common, neuter (**men**—masculine), third person, singular (**bells, sails, men**—plural), objective case, object of **have heard, saw, has lost, having sold, have seen, heard,** or **earned**, Rule VI.

Vice (3.) and **outrage** (7.)—nouns, common, neuter, third person, singular, nominative, Rule II.

Boys (4.), **vessel** (5.), **army** (9.), **words** (11.), and **man** (12.)—nouns, common (**vessel, words**—neuter; **boys, man**—masculine; **army**, common gender), third person, singular (**boys, words**—plural), nominative, Rule I.

Bay (5.), **Iowa** (6.), **darkness** and **solitude** (11.), **all, depravity, acquittal,** and **language** (12.), **reeds** and **crags** (13.), and **life** (14.)—nouns, common (**Iowa**—proper), neuter, third person, singular (**reeds, crags**—plural), objective case, used as the object of the prepositions **in, to, at, in, in, with, in, in, on,** and **through**, Rule VII.

General (9.) and **something** (both uses—14.)—nouns, common, (**general**—common gender; **something**—neuter), third person, singular, absolute case, it is part of the nominative absolute phrase, **the general having been captured,** or, **something attempted, something done**, Rule V.

14. **Night's**—noun, common, neuter, third person, singular, possessive, modifies **repose**, Rule III.

Pronouns—**I**—pronoun, personal, simple, its antecedent is the name, understood, of the speaker; gender, first person, singular to agree with its antecedent, Rule IX; nominative, Rule I.

2. **He**—pronoun, personal, simple, its antecedent is the name, understood, of the person spoken of; masculine, third person, singular, Rule IX; nominative, Rule I.

5. **Her**—pronoun, personal simple, its antecedent is **vessel**; feminine, third person, singular, Rule IX; possessive, modifies **sails**, Rule III.

6. **My**—pronoun, personal, simple, its antecedent is the name, understood, of the speaker; gender, first person, singular to agree with its antecedent, Rule IX; possessive, modifies **farm**, Rule III.

I—pronoun (parsed like **I** in sentence 1).

8. **You**—pronoun, personal, simple, its antecedent is the name, understood, of the person spoken to; gender unknown, second person, number unknown to agree with its antecedent, Rule IX; nominative, Rule I.

10. **Your**—pronoun, personal, simple, its antecedent is the name, understood, of the person spoken to; gender unknown, second person, number unknown to agree with its antecedent, Rule IX; posessive, modifies the participle **remaining**, which is the subject of **would ruin**, Rule III.

Us—pronoun, personal, simple, its antecedent is the name, understood, of the speakers, common gender, first person, plural, Rule IX; objective, object of **would ruin**, Rule VI.

11. **Me**—pronoun, personal, simple, its antecedent is the name understood, of the speaker; gender unknown, first person, singular to agree with its antecedent, Rule IX; objective, object of **before**, Rule VII.

13. **I**—pronoun, (parsed like **I** in sentence 1).

Adjectives—7. **Wanton**—adjective, descriptive (**wanton, more wanton, most wanton**), positive, belongs to **outrage**, Rule XII.

8. **Strong**—adjective, descriptive (**strong, stronger, strongest**), positive, belongs to **men**, Rule XII.

12. **Contented**—adjective, descriptive (**contented, more contented, most contented**), positive, belongs to **man**, Rule XII.

13. **Complete**—adjective, descriptive (**complete, more complete, most complete**), positive, belongs to **acquittal**, Rule XII.

N.B. Contented *and* **complete** *are adjectives which can be best understood by reflecting that both their verb forms are transitive, requiring objects (eg.* **He has contented himself; He will complete the task**). *The perfect participle of the verb* **complete**

is completed. Contented, *as a perfect/past participle, indicates past time or action, as do all other perfect/past participles* (*eg.* Contented, the man left—*participle*; *but,* He will be contented when he learns the truth—*adjective*; *or,* He contented himself with what he could learn—*verb transitive*).

Gracious—adjective, descriptive (**gracious, more gracious, most gracious**), positive belongs to language, Rule XII.

13. Wild—adjective, descriptive (**wild, wilder, wildest**), positive, belongs to **water**, Rule XII.

Participles—1.—Tolling—participle, derived from the verb **toll**, present participle, belongs to **bells**, Rule XII.

2. Opened—participle, derived from **open**, perfect/past participle, denotes completion, belongs to **letter**, Rule XII.

N.B. *The* **perfect participle** *is called the* **past participle** *by many grammarians.*

3. Gambling—participle noun/gerund, derived from **gamble**, neuter, third person, singular, nominative, Rule I.

4. Running, Jumping, and skating—participle nouns/gerunds, derived from the verbs **run, jump,** and **skate**, neuter, third person, singular, objective, object of **like**, Rule VI.

5. Anchored—participle, derived from the verb **anchor**, perfect/past particple, denotes completion, belongs to **vessel**, Rule XII.

6. Having sold—participle, derived from the verb **sell**, compound, denotes completion, belongs to **I**, Rule XII.

7. Burning—participle noun/gerund, derived from the verb **burn**, neuter, third person, singular, nominative, Rule I.

8. Weeping—participle, derived from the verb **weep**, present, denotes continuance, belongs to **men**, Rule XII.

9. Having been captured—participle, derived from the verb **capture**, compound, belongs to **general**, Rule XII.

10. Remaining—participle, derived from the verb **remain**, present, denotes continuance, belongs to **your**, Rule XII.

11. Said (both uses)—participles, derived from the verb **say**, perfect/past, denotes completion, belongs to **words**, Rule XII.

Marked—participle, derived from the verb **mark**, perfect/past, denotes completion, belongs to **words**, Rule XII.

12. Hardened—participle, derived from the verb **harden**, perfect/past, denotes completion, belongs to **man**, Rule XII.

Done—participle, derived from the verb **do**, perfect/past, denotes completion, belongs to **something**, Rule XII.

13. Washing—participle, derived from the verb **wash**, present/past, denotes continuance, belongs to **ripple**, Rule XII.

Lapping—participle, derived from the verb **lap**, present/past, denotes continuance, belongs to **water**, Rule XII.

Toiling, rejoicing, sorrowing—participles, derived from the verbs **toil, rejoice,** or **sorrow**, present, denotes continuance, belongs to **he**, Rule XII.

Attempted—participle, derived from the verb **attempt**, perfect/past, denotes completion, belongs to **something**, Rule XII.

Page 66
100. EXERCISES
Tell the mode of the verbs:

1. Ind.; **2.** pot.; **3.** imp.; **4.** imp.; **5.** sub., pot.; **6.** sub., ind., ind.; **7.** sub., pot.; **8.** ind.; **9.** let—imp., (to) see—inf.; **10.** pot.; **11.** imp.; **12.** are—ind., is—ind.; **13.** pot.; **14.** ind.; **15.** let—imp., beseech—imd., (to) deceive—inf.; **16.** help—imp., would be—pot.; **17.** if . . . is—sub., is—ind.; **18.** if . . . intersect—sub., will be—ind.; **19.** could have kept—sub., had been pot.; **20.** reign—imp., let—imp., (to) serve—inf.; **21.** place—imp., may hear—pot., (to) sweep—inf., let—imp., (to) sing—inf., (to) die—inf.

Page 82.
119. EXERCISES
Write a synopsis of the transitive verbs **write** et al.

The synopsis of a verb is the corrent arrangement of its modes/moods, voices, and tenses in one person and number. The synopsis is an abbreviated conjugation. For the purposes of this assignment, the student should copy the synopsis sections of **to love**, active and passive voices, sections 115 and 116, pages 75 and 77-82, supplying the correct forms of verbs chosen from the list in 119, page 82. Coordinate forms (section 117) may also be added for extra study. It is recommended that each student choose a different verb.

As an oral exercise, tell the mode, tense, person, and number of each verb:

1. **He has gone**—indicative, present perfect tense, second person, singular.

2. **I might write**—potential, past tense, first person, singular.

3. **We had gone**—indicative, past perfect, first person, plural.

4. **He had been assured**—indicative, past perfect, third person, singular.

5. **If I were loved**—subjunctive, past, first person, singular.

6. **They may have been left**—potential, present perfect, third person, plural.

7. **You were seen**—indicative, past, second person, plural.

8. **You will have loved**—indicative, future, second person, plural.

9. **She will have been invited**—indicative, future perfect, third person, singular.

10. **He night have built**—potential, past perfect, third person, singular.

11. **You might have been seen**—potential, past perfect, second person, plural.

12. **The ship will have sailed**—indicative, future perfect, third person, singular.

13. **We might have written**—potential, past perfect, first person, plural.

14. **They were loved**—indicative, past, third person, plural.

15. **If I had been loved**—subjunctive, past perfect, first person, singular.

16. **If he is loved**—indicative, present, third person, singular.

17. **Though he love**—subjunctive, present, third person, singular.

18. **Though he is loved**—indicative, present, third person, singular.

19. **If I may be seen**—subjunctive, present, first person, singular.

20. **We can go**—potential, present, first person, plural.

21. **Go**—imperative, present, second person, singular or plural.

22. **Remain**—imperative, present, second person, singular or plural.

23. **If he return**—subjunctive, present, third person, singular.

24. **If he returns**—indicative, present, third person, singular.

Pages 87-88

Parse the nouns, pronouns, adjectives, and verbs:

Nouns—1. **Plowing**—noun, participle, derived from the verb **plow**, neuter, third person, singular, objective, object of **commenced**, Rule VI.

2. **Letters**—noun, common, neuter, third person, plural, objective, the object of **write**, Rule VI.

3. **Father**—noun, common, masculine, third person, singular, nominative, Rule I.

Pineapples—noun, common, neuter, third person, plural, objective, the object of **bought**, Rule VI.

City—noun, common, neuter, third person, singular, objective, the object of the preposition **from**, Rule VII.

5. **To return**—noun, infinitive, neuter, third person, singular, objective, object of **intend**, Rule VI.

Umbrella—noun, common, neuter, third person, singular, objective, object of **to return**, Rule VI.

Workmen (6.), **name** (7.), **weather** (10.), **regiments** (13.), **professions** (16.), **goodness** (17.), **law** (18.—both uses), **parts, Bacon** (20.), and **goodness, weariness** (21.)—nouns, common (**Bacon**—proper), neuter (**Bacon, workmen**—masculine), third person, singular (**regiments, workmen, professions, parts**—plural), nominative, Rule I.

Aged (8.), **gifts** (14.), **creator** (15.), **prayer, footsteps** (17.), **tear, earth, planets** (18.), and **praise** (19.)—nouns, common (**Creator**—proper), neuter (**Creator**—masculine), third person, singular (**gifts, footsteps, planets**—plural), objective, the object of **respect, have, remember, hear, hath attended, molds, preserves, guides**, or **sing**, Rule VI.

Healing (14.), **days, youth** (15.), **source, course** (18.), **mankind** (20.), and **heart** (21.),—nouns, common, neuter (**youth, mankind**—common gender), third person, singular (**days**—plural), the object of the preposition **of, in, of, from, in, of**, or **to**, Rule VII.

17. **Father**—noun, common, masculine, second person, singular, absolute case, Rule V.

18. **Sphere**—noun, common, neuter, third person, singular, objective case, in apposition with **earth**, Rule IV.

19. **Soul**—noun, common, common gender, second person, singular, absolute case, Rule V.

God, Savior, King—nouns, proper (**king**—common), third person, singular, nominative, used as the predicate of **Who is thy God** . . . , Rule II.

Pronouns—1. **They**—pronoun, personal, third person, simple, its antecedent is the name, understood, of the person spoken of; gender, third person, plural to agree with its antecedent, Rule IX; nominative, Rule I.

2. **I**—pronoun, personal, first person, simple, its antecedent is the name understood, of the person speaking; gender unknown, first person, singular to agree with its antecedent, Rule IX; nominative, Rule I.

3. **My**—pronoun, personal, its antecedent is the name, understood, of the speaker; unknown gender, first person, singular to agree with its antecedent, Rule IX; possessive case, Rule III.

Me—pronoun, personal, its antecedent is the name, understood, of the speaker; unknown gender, first person, singular to agree with its

PAGE 88

antecedent, Rule IX; objective, object of **bought**, Rule VI.

He—pronoun, personal, its antecedent is **father**; masculine, third person, singular to agree with its antecedent, Rule IX; nominative case, Rule I.

4. **She**—pronoun, personal, its antecedent is the name, understood, of the person spoken of; feminine, third person, singular to agree with its antecedent, Rule IX; nominative case, Rule I.

5. **You**—pronoun, personal, its antecedent is the name, understood, of the person spoken to; unknown gender, second person, singular to agree with its antecedent, Rule IX; nominative case, Rule I.

7. **Thy**—pronoun, personal, its antecedent is **Father (God)**; masculine, second person, singular to agree with its antecedent, Rule IX; possessive case, Rule III.

9. **I**—(Parsed the same as **I** in 2).

11. **He**—(Parsed the same as **he** in 3).

12. **I**—(Same as **2** and **9**).

You—pronoun, personal, its antecedent is the name, understood, of the person spoken of; unknown gender, third person, number unknown to agree with its antecedent, Rule IX; objective case, the object of **shall assist**, Rule VI.

14. **Everyone**—pronoun, compound, indefinite, its antecedent is the name understood, of the person spoken of; unknown gender, third person, singular to agree with its antecedent, Rule IX; nominative case, Rule I.

Note—**everyone, everybody, no one, nobody, anyone, anybody, someone, somebody, each, either, neither,** and **one** are indefinite, singular pronouns. They refer generally and indefinitely to some one thing or person, as; **Everyone should have his (not their) own toothbrush.**

15. **Thy** (both uses)—pronoun, simple, singular, its antecedent is the name, understood, of the person spoken to; unknown gender, second person, singular to agree with its antecedent, Rule IX; possessive, Rule III.

16. **We**—pronoun, simple, personal, its antecedent is the name, understood, of the person(s) speaking; unknown gender, first person, plural, Rule IX; nominative, Rule I.

His—pronoun, simple, personal, its antecedent is the name, understood, of the person spoken of; masculine, third person, singular, Rule IX; possessive, Rule III.

17. **Our** (both uses)—pronoun, simple, personal, its antecedent is the name, understood, of the speaker; common gender, first person, plural, Rule IX; possessive, Rule III.

Thy—pronoun, simple, personal, its antecedent is **Father**; masculine, second person, singular by its form, Rule IX; possessive, Rule III.

18. **That**—pronoun, relative, its antecedent is **law**; simple, neuter, third person, singular, Rule IX; nominative, Rule I.

It—pronoun, personal, simple, its antecedent is **tear**; neuter, third person, singular, Rule IX; objective, object of **bids**, Rule VI.

Its—pronoun, personal, simple, its antecedent is **tear**; neuter, third person, singular, Rule IX; possessive, Rule III.

Their—pronoun, personal, simple, its antecedent is **planets**; neuter, third person, plural, Rule IX; possessive, Rule III.

19. **My**—pronoun, personal, simple, its antecedent is the name, understood, of the speaker; gender unknown, first person, singular, Rule IX; possessive, Rule III.

Thou—pronoun, personal, simple, its antecedent is **soul**; neuter, second person, singular, Rule IX; nominative, Rule I.

Him—pronoun, personal, simple, its subsequent is **God**; masculine, third person, singular, Rule IX; objective, object of **of**, Rule VII.

Who—pronoun, relative, its antecedent is **Him**; simple, masculine, third person, singular, Rule IX; nominative case, Rule I.

Thy (all three uses)—parsed identically with **thy** in 15.

20. **Thee**—pronoun, personal, simple, its antecedent is the name, understood, of the person spoken to; common gender, second person, singular by its form, Rule IX; objective, object of **allure**, Rule VI.

21. **Him**—pronoun, personal, simple, its antecedent is the name, understood, of the person spoken of; masculine, third person, singular, Rule IX; objective, object of **lead**, Rule VI.

Adjectives—3. **Some**—adjective, definitive, indefinite pronominal, it cannot be compared; belongs to **pineapples**, Rule XII.

The (here, and in **6, 15, 18, 19,** and **20**)—adjective, definitive, definite article, it cannot be compared; belongs to **city, workmen, days, planets, praise,** or **wisest, brightest, meanest,** Rule XII.

6. **Careful**—adjective, descriptive (**careful, more careful, most careful**) positive, belongs to **workmen**, Rule XII.

7. **Hallowed**—adjective, descriptive (**hallowed, more hallowed, most hallowed**) positive, belongs to **name**, Rule XII.

10. **Unpleasant**—adjective, descriptive, (**unpleasant, more unpleasant, most unpleasant**), positive, belongs to **weather**, Rule XII.

11. **Industrious**—adjective, descriptive (**industrious, more industrious, most industrious**), comparative, belongs to **he**, Rule XII.

13. **Many**—adjective, definitive, indefinite pronominal (**many, more, most**), positive, belongs to **regiments**, Rule XII.

16. **Insincere**—adjective, descriptive (**insincere, more insincere, most insincere**), positive, belongs to **professions**, Rule XII.

18. **That**—adjective, definitive, demonstrative pronominal, it cannot be compared; belongs to **law**, Rule XII.

Very—adjective, definitive, indefinite pronominal, it cannot be compared; belongs to **law**, Rule XII. (**Very** here means **identical** or **same**, and as such is not compared. But, meaning **absolute** or **utter**; as, **the very truth**, it compares **very, verier, veriest**).

A—adjective, definitive, indefinite article, it cannot be compared; belongs to **sphere**, Rule XII.

19. **Restless**—adjective, descriptive (**restless, more restless, most restless**), positive, belongs to **thou**, understood, Rule XII. (This is an ellipsis, reading, **Why art thou restless, why art thou cast down, my soul?** The subsequent of **thou** is **soul**, and the verb is **art . . . art . . . cast**).

20. **Wisest, brightest, meanest**—adjectives, here used substansively as nouns in apposition with **Bacon**; as, "The poor ye have always with you."

Verbs—1. **Commenced**—verb, regular (**commence, -ed, -ed**), transitive, active voice, indicative mode, past tense, third person, plural, Rule XIII.

2. **Write**—verb, irregular (**write, wrote, written**), transitive, active, indicative, present, first person, singular, Rule XII.

3. **Brought**—verb, irregular (**bring, brought, brought**), transitive, active, indicative, past, third person, singular, Rule XIII.

Came—verb, irregular (**come, came, come**), intransitive, active, indicative, past, third person, singular, Rule XII.

4. **Had gone**—verb, irregular (**go, went, gone**), intransitive, indicative, past perfect, third person, singular, Rule XIII.

To walk—verb, regular (**walk, -ed, -ed**), infinitive used adverbially, depends upon **had gone**, Rule XVII.

5. **Do intend**—verb, regular (**intend, -ed, -ed**), transitive, active, interrogative form, indicative, present, second person, singular, Rule XIII.

To return—verb, regular (**return, -ed, -ed**), transitive, active, infinitive, present, object of **do intend**, Rule VI.

6. **Should have been**—verb, irregular (**be or am, was, been**), copulative, potential, past perfect, third person, plural, Rule XIII.

7. **Be**—verb, irregular (**be or am, was, been**), copulative, imperative, present, second person, singular, Rule XIII.

8. **Respect**—verb, regular (**respect, -ed, -ed**), transitive, active, imperative, second person, singular or plural, Rule XIII.

9. **Could learn**—verb, regular (**learn, -ed, -ed**), transitive, active, potential, past, first person, singular, Rule XIII.

to do—verb, irregular (**do, did, done**), transitive, active, infinitive, present tense, object of **could learn**, Rule VI.

10. **Was**—verb, irregular (**be or am, was, been**), copulative, indicative, past, third person, singular, Rule XIII.

11. **Should have been**—verb, irregular (**be or am, was, been**), copulative, potential, past perfect, third person, plural, Rule XIII.

12. **Shall assist**—verb, regular (**assist, -ed, -ed**), transitive, active, interrogative form, indicative mode, future, first person, singular, Rule XIII.

13. **Were mustered**—verb, regular (**muster, -ed, -ed**), intransitive, passive, indicative, past, third person, plural, Rule XIII.

14. **Does have**—verb, irregular (**have or has, had, have**), transitive, active, interrogative form, indicative mode, present, third person, singular, Rule XIII.

15. **Remember**—verb, regular (**remember, -ed, -ed**), transitive, active, imperative, present, second person, singular or plural, Rule XIII.

16. **Were convinced**—verb, regular (**convince, -ed, -ed**), transitive, passive, indicative, past, first person, plural, Rule XIII.

17. **Hear, hear**—verb, irregular (**hear, heard, heard**), transitive, active, imperative, present, second person, singular, Rule XII.

Hath attended—verb, regular (**attend, -ed, -ed**), transitive, active, ancient form, indicative, present perfect, third person, singular, Rule XIII.

18. **Molds and bids**—compound verb, regular (**mold, -ed, -ed**)/irregular (**bid, bid, bid or bidden**), transitive, active, indicative, present, third person, singular, Rule XIII.

(To) trickle—verb, regular (**trickle, -ed, -ed**), intransitive, active, infinitive, used adverbially to modify **bids**, Rule XVII.

Preserves and guides—compound verb, regular (**preserve, -ed, -ed**/**guide, -ed, -ed**), transitive, active, indicative, present, third person, singular, Rule XIII.

19. **Art** (understood)—verb, irregular (**be or am, was, been**), copulative, it connects **thou**,

understood, to **restless**; ancient form, indicative, present, second person, singular, Rule XIII.

Art (understood) cast—verb, irregular (**be** or **am, was, been/cast, cast, cast**), intransitive, passive, indicative, present, second person, singular, Rule XII.

(Note: *Downcast, an adjective, is formed by joining the adverb* **down** *to the verb* **cast**. **Cast** *is here a verb, and its understood helper,* **art** *is the ancient singular form of* **be**. *Their subject is* **thou**, *understood; as, Why art thou cast down?*).

Hope—verb, regular (**hope, -ed, -ed**), intransitive, active, imperative, present, second person, singular, Rule XIII.

Shalt sing—verb, irregular (**sing, sang, sung**), transitive, active, ancient form, indicative, future, second person, singular, Rule XIII.

Is—verb, irregular (**be** or **am, was, been**), copulative, it joins **who** to **God**; indicative, present, third person, singular, Rule XIII.

20. **Allure**—verb, regular (**allure, -ed, -ed**), transitive, active, subjunctive mode, present, third person, plural, Rule XIII.

Think—verb, irregular (**think, thought, thought**), intransitive, active, indicative, present, second person, singular, Rule XIII.

Shines—verb, regular or irregular (**shine, -ed, -ed**)/**shine, shone, shone**), transitive, active, indicative, past, third person, singular, Rule XIII.

21. **Lead**—verb, irregular (**lead, led, led**), transitive, active subjunctive, present, third person, singular, Rule XIII.

May toss—verb, regular (**toss, -ed, -ed**), transitive, active, potential, present, third person, singular, Rule XIII.

Page 88
Passive forms:

Nouns—1. **Stripes**—noun, common, neuter, third person, plural, objective, object of **with**, Rule VII.

2. **Sheep**—noun, common, common gender, third person, plural, nominative, Rule I.

Wolves—noun, common, common gender, third person, plural, objective, object of **by**, Rule VII.

3. **Crime**—noun, common, neuter, third person, singular, nominative, Rule I.

5. **America**—noun, proper, neuter, third person, singular, nominative, Rule I.

Christopher Columbus—noun, proper, masculine, third person, singular, objective, object of **by**, Rule VII.

6. **Mayor**—noun, common, masculine, third person, singular, objective, object of **has been elected**, Rule VI.

City—noun, common, neuter, third person, singular, objective, object of **of**, Rule VII.

7. **Work**—noun, common, neuter, third person, singular, nominative, Rule I.

Pronouns—1. **He** (here and in **4** and **6**)—pronouns, personal, simple, their antecedents are the names, understood, of the persons spoken of; masculine, third person, singular, Rule IX; nominative, Rule I.

4. **You**—pronoun, personal, simple, its antecedent is the name, understood, of the person(s) spoken to; unknown gender, second person, number unknown, Rule IX; nominative, Rule I.

I—pronoun, personal, simple, its antecedent is the name, understood, of the speaker; gender unknown, first person, singular, Rule IX; nominative, Rule I.

6. **Our**—pronoun, personal, simple, its antecedents are the names, understood, of the persons speaking; common gender, first person, plural, Rule IX; possessive, Rule III.

Adjective—1. **Many**—adjective, definitive, indefinite pronominal (**many, more, most**), positive, belongs to **stripes**, Rule XII.

2. **The** (also in 7)—adjective, definitive, definite article, cannot be compared, belongs to **sheep** or **work**, Rule XII.

3. **Every**—adjective, definitive, distributive pronominal, cannot be compared, belongs to **crime**, Rule XII.

Verbs—1. **Was beaten**—verb, irregular (**beat, beaten, beaten**), transitive, passive, indicative, past tense, third person, singular, Rule XII.

2. **Were destroyed**—verb, regular (**destroy, -ed, -ed**), transitive, passive, indicative, past, third person, plural, Rule XIII.

3. **Should be punished**—verb, regular (**punish, -ed, -ed**), transitive, passive, potential, present, third person, singular, Rule XIII.

4. **Were invited**—verb, regular (**invite, -ed, -ed**), transitive, passive, indicative, past, third person, plural, Rule XIII.

5. **Was discovered**—verb, regular (**discover, -ed, -ed**), transitive, passive, indicative, past, third person, singular, Rule XIII.

6. **Has been elected**—verb, regular (**elect, -ed, -ed**), transitive, passive, indicative, present perfect, third person, singular, Rule XIII.

7. **Might have been finished**—verb, regular (**finish, -ed, -ed**), transitive, passive, potential mode, past perfect, third person, singular, Rule XIII.

Progressive, Emphatic, and Interrogative forms:

Nouns—**1. Letter**—noun, common, neuter, third person, singular, objective, object of **is writing**, Rule VI.

2. Lessons—noun, common, neuter, third person, plural, objective, object of **should have been studying**, Rule VI.

3. Gold—noun, common, neuter, third person, singular, objective, object of **for**, Rule VII.

5. Forgery—noun, common, neuter, third person, singular, objective, object of **did commit**, Rule VI.

7. Denying—noun, participle, it is derived from the verb, **deny**; neuter, third person, singular, objective, object of **in**, Rule VII.

Pronouns—**1. He** (also in **5** and **7**)—pronouns, personal, simple, their antecedents are the names, understood, of the persons spoken of; masculine, third person, singular, Rule IX; nominative, Rule I.

2. They (also in **3**)—pronouns, personal, simple, their antecedents are the names, understood, of the persons spoken of; common gender, third person, plural, Rule IX; nominative, Rule I.

Their—pronoun, personal, simple, its antecedents are the names, understood, of the persons spoken of; common gender, third person, plural, Rule IX; possessive, Rule III.

4. I (also in **8**)—pronouns, personal, simple, their antecedents are the names, understood, of the speakers, common gender, first person, singular, Rule IX; nominative, Rule I.

You (also in **6** and the first clause of **8**)—pronouns, personal, simple, their antecedents are the names, understood, of the persons spoken to; common gender, second person, number unknown, Rule IX; nominative, Rule I.

Note: *Many grammarians perceive* **you** *as singular when the antecedent is unknown, or when the context may seem to indicate a singular number. But, as in the example above, more than one person may be spoken to in almost any context. One might* **wish you** *(parents, siblings, etc.)* **were here** *in plural as readily as singular.*

Some Elizabethan constructions get around this difficulty in the phrase **you all** *(cf. Phil. 1:8). This construction is retained by many speakers of the Southeastern U.S., though occasionally employed incorrectly in the singular.*

7. It—pronoun, personal, simple, its antecedent is the idea, understood, spoken of; neuter, third person, singular, Rule IX; objective, object of **denying**, Rule VI.

8. You (second use)—pronoun, personal, simple, its antecedent is the name, understood, of the person spoken to; common gender, second person, number unknown, Rule IX; objective, object of **met**, Rule VI.

Adjective—**1. A**—adjective, definitive, indefinite article, it cannot be compared; belongs to **letter**, Rule XII. (This is the only adjective in this exercise).

Verbs—**1. Is writing**—verb, irregular (**write, wrote, written**), transitive, active, progressive, indicative, present, third person, singular, Rule XIII.

2. Should have been studying—verb, regular (**study, studied, studied**), transitive, active, progressive, potential, past perfect, third person, plural, Rule XIII.

3. Were digging—verb, irregular (**dig, dug, dug**), transitive, active, progressive, indicative, past, third person, plural, Rule XIII.

4. Do wish—verb, irregular (**do, did, done**), transitive, emphatic form indicative, present, first person, singular, Rule XIII.

Were—verb, irregular (**be** or **am, was, been**), copulative, it is used in the sense of **exists**; intransitive, subjunctive, past, second person, number unknown, Rule XIII.

5. Did commit—verb, regular (**commit, committed, committed**), transitive, emphatic form, indicative, past, sesond person, singular, Rule XIII.

6. Do learn—verb, regular or irregular (**learn, -ed, -ed/learn, learnt, learnt**), intransitive, emphatic form, indicative, present, second person, singular or plural number, Rule XIII.

7. Does persist—verb, regular (**persist, -ed, -ed**), intransitive, emphatic form, indicative, present, third person, singular, Rule XIII.

8. Were going—verb, irregular (**go, went, gone**), intransitive, interrogative form indicative, past, second person, singular or plural, Rule XIII.

Met—verb, irregular (**meet, met, met**), transitive, active, indicative, past, first person, singular, Rule XIII.

Page 93-94
132. EXERCISES
Parse the adverbs:

1. Very—adverb; it is not compared; manner, modifies **happily**, Rule XVIII.

Happily—adverb (**happily, more happily, most happily**), manner, modifies **lived**, Rule XVIII.

2. Why—adverb, it is not compared; interrogative adverb of cause, modifies **do look**, Rule XVIII.

So—adverb, it is not compared, manner, modifies the adjective **sad**, Rule XVIII.

3. When—adverb, conjunctive, modifies **comes**, Rule XVIII.

PAGE 94-98

4. How—adverb, it is not compared; manner, modifies **rapidly**, Rule XVIII.

Rapidly—adverb (**rapidly, more rapidly, most rapidly**), manner, modifies **fly**, Rule XVIII.

5. Then and there—adverbial phrase, modifies **signed**, Rule XVIII.

6. Again and again—adverbial phrase, modifies **have read**, Rule XVIII.

7. So—adverb, it is not compared; manner, modifies **will do**.

No longer—adverbial phrase, modifies **will do**, Rule XVIII.

8. By and by—adverbial phrase of time, modifies **will be explained**, Rule XVIII.

9. Perhaps—adverb, modal, modifies the entire clause, **you are the man**, Rule XVIII.

10. Where—adverb, it is not compared; interrogative adverb of place, modifies **has gone**, Rule XVIII.

11. Agreeably—adverb (**agreeably, more agreeably, most agreeably**), manner, modifies **were disappointed**, Rule XVIII.

12. Over the hill—prepositional phrase used adverbially, place, modifies **lives**, Rule XVIII.

13. Henceforth—adverb, it is not compared; time, modifies **let fear**, Rule XVIII.

14. Before—adverb, it is not compared; conjunctive, joins two clauses, modifies **left**, Rule XVIII.

Note: Some grammarians treat **before** *as a subordinating conjunction in this usage, and view it as an adverb only when used as an adverb of time or place (eg.* **He went before; I've heard that tale before**). *Harvey's and the Plain English Handbook view it as a conjunction when it introduces a clause modifying the entire main clause (***I was here before you came.***) and as a conjunctive adverb when it introduces a clause which modifies the verb in the main clause (***Dick came before we left***). The difference here is so slight and subtle that the designation "conjunctive adverb" is probably useful only to point out the adverbial function of subordinators as modifiers as well as joiners. Oxford designates* **before** *as a "conjunction or conjunctive adverb."*

15. Not—adverb, it is not compared; manner, modifies **will be**, Rule XVIII.

16. Not—adverb, it is not compared; modifies **have seen**, Rule XVIII.

Since—adverb, it is not compared; conjunctive, modifies **returned**, Rule XVIII.

(**Since**, like **before**, when used to join clauses, is treated as a conjunction by some grammarians).

From New York—adverbial prepositional phrase, modifies **returned**, Rule XVIII.

17. Doubtless—adverb, (**doubtless, more doubtless, most doubtless**), modal, it modifies the entire clause; Rule XVIII.

("Words like **not, perhaps,** and **certainly**, which, instead of modifying a single word, change or modify the meaning of the entire sentence, are called **modal adverbs**"—Patterson).

18. Perhaps—adverb, it is not compared; modal, it modifies **I shall go**, Rule XVIII.

Page 98
139. EXERCISES
Parse the prepositions:

1. With—preposition, it shows the relation between **me** and **go**; Rule XIX.

Into—preposition, it shows the relation between **garden** and **go**; Rule XIX.

2. In—preposition, it shows the relation between **house** and **mansions**; Rule XIX.

3. Over—preposition, it shows the relation between **river** and **went**; Rule XIX.

Through—preposition, it shows the relation between **cornfields** and **went**; Rule XIX.

Into—preposition, it shows the relation between **woods** and **went**; Rule XIX.

4. As to—complex preposition, it shows the relation between **affair** and **am satisfied**; Rule XIX.

5. But—preposition, it shows the relation between **Mary** and **all**.

6. From among—complex preposition, it shows the relation between **Alps** and **flows**; Rule XIX.

(**Out** is in this sentence as an adverb modifying **flows**, apart from the prepositional phrase).

7. From—preposition, it shows the relation between **St. Louis** and **went**; Rule XIX.

Across—preposition, it shows the relation between **plains** and **went**; Rule XIX.

Over—preposition, it shows the relation between **Rockies** and **went**; Rule XIX.

To—preposition, it shows the relation between **California** and **went**; Rule XIX.

8. In, in, from, of—prepositions, they show the relation between **lines, directions, point,** or **emission,** and **light**; Rule XIX.

9. Aboard—preposition, it shows the relation between **ship** and **went**; Rule XIX.

10. From, in, o'er—prepositions, they show the relation between **throne, majesty,** or **world,** and the verb **stretches**; Rule XIX.

Correct the following:
1. Between; 2. within the next week; 3. to; 4. into; 5. connect; 6. from (out of is archaic); **7. on** (or substitute the preposition and article for **one**); **8.** omit **to; 9. upon** (or correct); **10. of** (or correct); **11. at; 12. by; 13. to make; 14. of; 15. by** (or delete **accompanied**); **16. by; 17. from**.

Page 102

146. EXERCISES

Parse . . . the following:

(Here we have parsed all the conjunctions and named the part of speech of all the words in this exercise).

1. **He**—pronoun.
   'd (would) . . . die . . . ask—verb.
   Sooner—adverb.
   Than—conjunction.
   You—pronoun.
   For—preposition.
   A—adjective.
   Shilling—noun.
2. **Talent**—noun.
   Is—verb.
   Something—noun.
   But—conjunction.
   Tact—noun.
   Is—verb.
   Everything—noun.
3. **Neither . . . nor**—conjunctions.
   Military—adjective.
   Civil—adjective.
   Pomp—noun.
   Was—verb.
   Wanting—adjective (participle).
4. **The**—adjective.
   Truth—noun.
   That—conjunction.
   I—pronoun.
   Am tired—verb.
   Of—preposition.
   Ticking—noun (gerund/participle).
5. **I**—pronoun.
   Remember—verb.
   A—adjective.
   Mass—noun.
   Of—preposition.
   Things—noun.
   But—conjunction.
   Nothing—noun.
   Distinctly—adverb.
6. **I**—pronoun.
   Was—verb.
   Solitary—adjective.
   And—conjunction.
   Idle—adjective.
7. **Both . . . and**—conjunctions.
   The—adjective.
   Ties—noun.
   Of—preposition.
   Nature—noun.
   The—adjective.
   Dictates—noun.
   Of—preposition.
   Policy—noun.
   Demand—verb.
   This—pronoun.
8. **There**—adverb (used as an anticipatory subject).
   Was—verb.
   No—adjective.
   Reply—noun.
   For—conjunction.
   Fear—noun.
   Was—verb.
   Upon—preposition.
   Every—adjective.
   Man—noun.
9. **No**—adjective.
   Man—noun.
   More—adverb.
   Highly—adverb.
   Esteems—verb.
   Or—conjunction.
   Honors—verb.
   The—adjective.
   British—adjective.
   Troops—noun.
   Than—conjunction.
   I—pronoun.
   Do—verb.
10. **The**—adjective.
    Soldier—noun.
    Marches—verb.
    On and on—compound adverb.
    Inflicting—adjective (participle).
    Pain—noun.
    And—conjunctin.
    Suffering—noun.
    As—conjunction.
    Before—adverb (used modally).
11. **There**—adverb.
    May be—verb.
    Wisdom—noun.
    With—preposition.
    Knowledge—noun.
    And—conjunction.
    There—adverb.
    May be—verb.
    Knowledge—noun.
    Without—preposition.
    Wisdom—noun.
12. **Not**—adverb (used modally).
    A—adjective.
    Having—noun (gerund).
    And—conjunction.
    Resting—noun (gerund).
    But—conjunction.

PAGE 102

 A—adjective.
 Growing—noun (gerund).
 And—conjunction.
 Becoming—noun (gerund).
 Is—verb.
 The—adjective.
 True—adjective.
 Character—noun.
 Of—preposition.
 Perfection—noun.
 As—conjunction.
 Culture—noun.
 Conceives—verb.
 It—pronoun.
13. **Men**—noun.
 Must be taught—verb.
 As if—conjunction.
 You—pronoun.
 Taught—verb.
 Them—pronoun.
 Not—adverb.
14. **Essex**—noun.
 Had—verb.
 Neither . . . nor—conjunction.
 The—adjective.
 Virtues—noun.
 The—adjective.
 Vices—noun.
 Which—pronoun.
 Enable—verb.
 Men—noun.
 To retain—verb.
 Greatness—noun.
 Long—adverb.
15. **How**—adverb.
 Long—adverb.
 Didst think—verb.
 Thou—pronoun.
 That—conjunction.
 His—pronoun.
 Silence—noun.
 Was—verb.
 Slumber—noun.
16. **Vice**—noun.
 Is—verb.
 A—adjective.
 Monster—noun.
 Of—preposition.
 So—adverb.
 frightful—adjective.
 Mein—noun.
 As—conjunction.
 To be hated—verb.
 Needs—verb.
 But—conjunction.

 To be seen—verb.
 Too—adverb.
 Oft—adverb.
 Familiar—adjective (modifies **we**, to which it is joined by the understood copula, **having become**, in this ellipsis).
 With—preposition.
 Her—pronoun.
 Face—noun.
 We—pronoun.
 First—adverb.
 Endure—verb.
 Then—adverb.
 Pity—verb.
 Then—adverb.
 Embrace—verb.

Conjunctions—1. **Than**—conjunction, subordinate of degree, it connects **die** and **ask**; Rule XXI.

2. **But**—conjunction, coordinate, adversative, it connects two equal clauses; Rule XX.

3. **Neither . . . nor**—coordinate, correlative, it connects **military** and **civil**; Rule XX.

4. **That**—conjunction, subordinate, it joins **tired** with **truth**; Rule XXI.

5. **But**—conjunction, coordinate, it joins two clauses (the second is elliptical); Rule XX.

6. **And**—conjunction, coordinate, it joins **solitary** and **idle**; Rule XX.

7. **Both . . . and**—conjunction, coordinate, correlative, it joins **ties** and **dictates**; Rule XX.

8. **For**—conjunction, coordinating, it joins two equal clauses; Rule XX.

9. **Or**—conjunction, coordinating, it joins **esteems** and **honors**; Rule XX.

 Than—conjunction, subordinating of manner; it connects the main clause with **I do**; Rule XXI.

10. **And**—conjunction, coordinating; it joins **pain** and **suffering**; Rule XX.

11. **And**—conjunction, coordinating, it joins two equal clauses; Rule XX.

12. **And** (both uses)—conjunction, coordinating, it joins **having** and **resting**/**growing** and **becoming**; Rule XX.

 But—conjunction, coordinating, it joins two equal compound subjects; Rule XX.

 As—conjunction, subordinating, it joins the main clause to a subordinate clause; Rule XXI.

13. **As if**—conjunction, correlative, subordinate, it joins two unequal clauses; Rule XXI.

14. **Neither . . . nor**—conjunction, correlative, coordinating, it joins **virtues** and **vices**; Rule XX.

15. **That**—conjunction, subordinating, it joins a main clause to a subordinate clause; Rule XXI.

16. **As**—conjunction, subordinate, it joins the

adjective infinitive phrase **to be hated** to **monster**; Rule XXI.

(**But**, in the first use is an adverb, synonymous with **merely** or **only**, modifying the verb **needs**, whose elliptical subject is **vice**. **To be seen** is the object of **needs**).

But (second use)—conjunction, subordinating, it joins the participle adjective **seen** to **monster**; Rule XXI.

Page 104
151 EXERCISES
Parse . . . the words:
1. **Ha**—interjection.
   Laughest—verb.
   Thou—pronoun.
2. **Hey**—interjection.
   Sirs—noun.
   What—adjective.
   A—adjective.
   Noise—noun.
   You—pronoun.
   Make—verb.
   Here—adverb.
3. **Hurrah, hurrah**—interjection.
   Long—adverb.
   Live—verb.
   Lord Robin—noun.
4. **Hah**—interjection.
   It—pronoun.
   Is—verb.
   A—adjective.
   Sight—noun.
   To freeze—verb (used as an adjective).
   One—pronoun.
5. **Let . . . be**—verb.
   Them—pronoun.
   Desolate—adjective.
   For—preposition.
   A—adjective.
   Reward—noun.
   Of—preposition.
   Their—pronoun.
   Shame—noun.
   Which—pronoun.
   Say—verb.
   Unto—preposition.
   Me—pronoun.
   Aha, aha—interjection.
6. **Oh**—interjection.
   That—conjunction.
   The—adjective.
   Salvation—noun.
   Of—preposition.
   Israel—noun.
   Were come—verb.
   Out of—preposition.
   Zion—noun.
7. **Alas**—interjection.
   All—adjective.
   Earthly—adjective.
   Good—noun.
   Still—adverb.
   Blends—verb.
   Itself—pronoun.
   With—preposition.
   Home—noun.
8. **Tush, tush**—interjection.
   Man—noun.
   I—pronoun.
   Made—verb.
   No—adjective.
   Reference—noun.
   To—preposition.
   You—pronoun.
9. **Hark**—interjection.
   What—adjective.
   Nearer—adjective.
   War—adjective.
   Drum—noun.
   Shakes—verb.
   The—adjective.
   Gale—noun.
10. **Soft**—interjection.
    I—pronoun.
    Did dream—verb.
    But—adverb.
11. **What**—interjection.
    Old—adjective.
    Acquaintance—noun.
    Could keep—verb.
    Not—adverb.
    All—adjective.
    This—adjective.
    Flesh—noun.
    In—adverb.
    A—adjective.
    Little—adjective.
    Life—noun.
    Poor—adjective.
    Jack—noun.
    Farewell—interjection. (Separated by a comma from **Jack**, **farewell** is here an interjection, rather than the predicate of a clause. **Jack** is therefore absolute, rather than nominative.
    I—pronoun.
    Could have spared—verb.
    Better—adverb (first usage).
    A—adjective.

PAGE 104-109

>Better—adjective (second usage).
>Man—noun.

The interjections are here parsed:
>**Ha** (1.), **hey** (2.), **hurrah, hurrah** (3.), **hah** (4.), **aha, aha** (5.), **oh** (6.), **alas** (7.), **tush, tush** (8.), **hark** (9.), **soft** (10.), **what** and **farewell** (11.), are interjections. They denote strong emotion. Rule XXII: "An interjection has no dependance upon other words.".

Pages 104-106
152. MISCELLANEOUS EXERCISES.

Here is a selection of sentences, some from classical literature, which the teacher may wish to use for parsing or diagramming assignments, on paper or on the board, to aid students who need extra help.

PART III
SYNTAX
Page 108
LESSON I
Affirm qualities of the following subjects: (Answers may vary)
>**Iron** is strong.
>**Gold** is yellow.
>**Silver** is soft.
>**Lead** is heavy.
>**Ink** is black.
>**Cork** is light.
>**Sugar** is sweet.
>**Vinegar** is sour.
>**Grass** is green.
>**Books** are printed.
>**Lessons** are to be learned.

Affirm the following qualities of appropriate subjects.
>Cellophane is **transparent.**
>Black paint is **opaque.**
>Diamond is **hard.**
>Hail is **round.**
>Blocks are **square.**
>Virtue is **good.**
>Decay is **bad.**
>Brussel sprouts are **bitter.**
>Bricks are **heavy.**
>The road is **rough.**
>Glass is **smooth.**
>Blood is **red.**
>Dandelions are **yellow.**
>Firs are **green.**

Class: Horses are draft animals.
Qualities: Horses are strong.

Class: Oxen are cattle.
Qualities: Oxen are gentle.

Class: Coal is a fossil.
Qualities: Coal is black.

Class: Wood is cellulose.
Qualities: Wood is fibrous.

Class: Hay is fodder.
Qualities: Hay is flammable.

Class: Oats are grain.
Qualities: Oats are edible.

Class: Wheat is a crop.
Qualities: Wheat is hardy.

Class: An ax is a tool.
Qualities: An ax should be sharp.

Class: A hoe is an implement.
Qualities: A hoe is useful.

Class: A locomotive is a vehicle.
Qualities: A locomotive is powerful.

Class: Dogs are canine.
Qualities: Dogs are bold.

Class: Sheep are livestock.
Qualities: Sheep are timid.

Class: Copper is a metal.
Qualities: Copper is yellow.

Class: Gold is precious.
Qualities: Gold is soft.

Class: Apples are fruit.
Qualities: Many apples are tart.

Class: Trees are plants.
Qualities: Trees may be tall.

Class: Wagons are conveyances.
Qualities: Wagons are slow.

Class: Houses are dwellings.
Qualities: Houses should be comfortable.

Page 109
Write sentences, using these verbs:
>(The teacher should point out that, though of

only two words, these are **complete** sentences, since each has a **subject** and a **verb**. A word group is not a sentence, no matter how many words it may contain, unless it contains **both** of these elements. Other word groups are called **fragments**.)

People **walk**.
Choirs **sing**.
Teakettles **whistle**.
Dolphins **swim**.
Boys **wrestle**.
Children **play**.
Students **write**.
Scholars **study**.
Farmers **plow**.
Laborers **reap**.
Truckers **drive**.
Ponies **neigh**.
Geese **cackle**.
Tires **whine**.
Dogs **snarl**.
Turkeys **gobble**.
Starlings **quarrel**.
Cats **fight**.

LESSON IV
EXERCISES

1. **Ink**—subject, of which something is affirmed. **Black**—predicate, which is afffirmed of the subject. **Is**—copula.

(All other sentences in this exercise follow this pattern exactly, except that several have no copula.)

Page 110

The students should prepare brief subject-verb-object sentences for their own analysis, then analyze them. The teacher may wish to check each student's work before asking him to proceed. The sample given in the text—**Children love play**—and the analyzed sentences below, should provide the teacher with sufficient examples. Refer back to the models on page **10** for more detailed analysis.

Analyze also the following sentences:

1. **Heat**, subject; **melts**, the predicate, modified by **lead**, its object.

2. **Men**, subject; **love**, the predicate, modified by **money**, the object of **love**.

3. **I**, subject; **study**, the predicate. **Botany** is the object of **study**.

4. **Haste**, subject; **makes**, the predicate, modified by the noun **waste**, its object.

5. **Cats**, subject; **catch**, predicate, modified by **mice**, object.

6. **Mr. Jones**, subject; **sells** predicate, modified by **encyclopedias**, object.

7. **Clouds**, subject; **bring**, predicate, modified by **rain**, the direct object.

Page 111

Analyze the following sentences:

1. **Book**, subject; **lost**, the predicate; **book**, is modified by **Sarah's**, and **is** is the copula.

2. **Mrs. Elkins**, subject; **found**, predicate. **Mrs. Elkins** is modified by **seamstress**, its appositive, and **seamstress** by **the**, an adjective. **Book**, object, modifies **found**; and **Sarah's** modifies **book**.

3. **People**, subject; **love**, the predicate; **quiet** is the object and modifier. **Old**, an adjective, modifies **people**.

4. **Children**, subject; **love**, the predicate; **play** is its object and modifier. **Young**, an adjective, modifies **children**.

5. **I**, subject; **like**, the predicate; **cherries**, its object, modified by **ripe**, an adjective.

6. **You**, subject; **have found**, predicate. **Pencil**, object, modifies **have found**, and **my** modifies **pencil**.

Page 112
EXERCISES

1. **Sluggard**, subject; **sleeps**, the predicate. **Sluggard** is modified by **a**, an adjective; **sleeps** is modified by **soundly**, an adverb.

2. **Horses**, subject; **were fatigued**, predicate. **Horses** is modified by **the**, an adjective; **were fatigued** is modified by **much**, an adverb.

3. **Reports**, subject; **were heard**, predicate. **Loud**, an adjective, modifies **reports**, and the adverb **very** modifies **loud**.

4. **Boy**, subject; **spends**, predicate. The object of **spends** is **money**, which is modified by **his**. **Foolishly**, an adverb, modified the verb **spends**.

5. **You**, subject; **may go**, predicate. **Now**, adverb, modifies the verb **may go**.

6. **He**, subject; **left**, predicate, modified by **then**, an adverb. **Country** is the object, modified by **the**, an adjective.

7. **River**, subject; **rose**, predicate, modified by **rapidly**, an adverb. **The**, adjective, modifies **river**.

8. **Troops**, subject; **marched**, predicate, modified by **forward**, an adverb. **The**, adjective, modifies **troops**.

9. **Parents**, subject; **live**, predicate, modified by **there**, an adverb. **Their**, a pronoun, is used adjectively to modify **parents**.

10. **Horses**, subject; **did run**, predicate, modified by **far**, an adverb, which in turn is modified by **how**, another adverb. **The**, adjective, modifies **horses**.

11. **He**, subject; **acted**, predicate, modified by **wisely**, an adverb.

12. **Mr. Mason**, subject; **man**, predicate, which is joined to the subject by the copula, **is**. **Good**, adjective, modifies **man**; and **truly**, an adverb, modifies **good**.

13. **He**, subject; **will be heard**, predicate, modified by the adverbs **from** and **presently**.

14. **Men**, subject; **were fatigued**, predicate, modified by **much**, an adverb, in turn modified by **very**, another adverb. **The**, adjective, modifies **men**.

15. **Doctor**, subject; **will be** is the predicate. **Here**, a modal adverb, modifies the entire proposition, **doctor will be here**. **Immediately**, an adverb, modifies **here**. **The**, adjective, modifies the subject, **doctor**.

Page 114
156. EXERCISES
Tell to which class each belongs:
Declarative—**1, 3, 5, 7, 13, 16,** and **18**.
Interrogative—**2, 9,** and **17**.
Imperative—**4, 12,** and **15**.
Exclamatory—**6, 8, 10, 11,** and **14**.

Page 116
159. EXERCISES

1, 2, 3, 4, 5, 7, 8, 9, 10, 15, 17, 18, and **20** are sentences, declarative, simple. Number **17** may also be taken as compound. The subject of **lead** is **Thou**, understood. **Deliver** may therefore be perceived either as part of a compound verb—**lead . . . but deliver**—or part of another clause with a second **Thou**, understood, as its subject.

6. Sentence, exclamatory, simple.

11. Sentence, declarative, complex; it is composed of two clauses. The principal clause is **The village all declared**, and the subordinate or dependent clause is **how much he knew**, an objective noun clause, object of **declared**, which it modifies.

12. Sentence, declarative, complex; it is composed of two clauses. The principal clause is **he . . . despiseth his own soul**, and the subordinate/dependent clause is **that refuseth instruction**, which adjectively modifies **he** in the main clause.

13. Sentence, interrogative, complex. **Is it**, the principal clause, is used idiomatically to introduce the dependent clause, **the lark ascends and sings**. **For thee**, an adverbial element, acts modally to modify **is it**. **Does the lark ascend and sing for thee?** is a reduction of this complex sentence to its essential elements.

14. Sentence, exclamatory, compound. **This place is dreadful** and **God is here** are joined by the coordinate conjunction **for**. **How**, an adverb, modifies the adjective **dreadful** in the first clause; **dreadful**, in turn, modifies **place**. **Here**, a modal adverb, modifies the entire second clause.

16. Sentence, interrogative, simple. **For the loss**, an adverbial prepositional phrase, modifies the verb, **can compensate**, and the adjective prepositional phrase, **of character** modifies **loss**.

19. Sentence, exclamatory, complex. **All were sealed** is the main clause. **With the seal**, an adverbial prepositional phrase, modifies **sealed**, the verb. **Which**, a relative pronoun, introduces the adjective clause **which is to be broken**, modifying **seal**. **Never**, an adverb, modifies the infinitive **to be broken**; **till the great day**, an adverbial prepositional phrase, modifies **to be broken**.

21. Sentence, imperative, compound-complex. The coordinate clauses are **(you)**, understood, **talk to the point** and and **(you) stop**. The conjunctive adverb **when** joins the subordinate clause, **you have reached it**, to the main clauses, which it modifies.

22. Sentence, declarative, compound-complex. The coordinate clauses are **It was now the Sabbath day** and **a small congregation . . . had met**. **It**, the subject of the first clause, is used idiomatically to introduce the sentence, the real subject being **Sabbath day**. **Now**, an adverb, modifies the entire clause. **Of about a hundred souls**, adjective prepositional phrase, modifies **congregation**. The adverbial prepositional phrases **for divine service** and **in a place** modify the verb **had met**, in the second clause. **Magnificient**, an adjective, modifies **place**; and **more**, an adverb, modifies **magnificient**.

Than, a conjunction, joins and compares **place** and **temple**, the subject of the elliptical clause, **any temple is magnificient**.

That, pronoun, introduces the relative clause, **human hands had ever built**, which modifies **temple**. **Ever**, adverb, modifies **had built**, as does the adverbial phrase, **to Deity**.

23. Sentence, declarative, compound-complex. The main clause is **I know**. **(That) thou art gone** is a noun clause, the object of **know**, verb of the main clause.

Where the weary are blest and **and (where) the mourner looks up and is glad** are subordinate clauses adverbially modifying **art gone**.

24. Sentence, interrogative, complex. The main clauses in both are **What (did it) matter**. **What** is here used adverbially meaning **in what respect**. **Matter**, here a verb, signifies **to be of importance**. **It**, understood, is the subject, and its verb is **did**, understood, **matter**.

How the night behaved and **how the north wind raved** are both here subordinate clauses introduced by the conjunction **how**, meaning **the manner in which**. (Quote is from Whittier's *Snowbound*.)

25. Sentence, declarative, compound-complex. **Bird**, a noun used absolutely, is modified by the adjective prepositional phrase, **of the broad and sweeping wing**. **Home** is the subject of the main clause; **is**, the copula, connects it to its modifier, **high**, modified by **in heaven**. The remainder, **where ... driven**, consists of two adjective clauses modifying **heaven**.

Page 118
162. EXERCISES IN ANALYSIS

All sentences in this exercise are declarative. All are simple except number **26** which is compound. The first word of all 38 sentences (**Children, virtue, spring**, etc.) is the subject, except that in number **26** the first word of each clause is the subject of the clause. These sentences are all arranged according to natural order.

Sentences **1-12** have no copulas. In each case the first word is the subject, and the rest of the words are the predicate, which is affirmed of the subject.

In sentences **13-38** the final word in each sentence (clause, number **26**) is the predicate, which in every case is either an adjective modifying the subject (eg. **metal, insects**). All words between the subject and the predicate in these sentences are copulas, joining the two.

Page 119
164. EXERCISES IN SYNTHESIS
Affirm actions:

In this exercise the student, using the models, is to couple any appropriate action verb to the stated noun subjects. All four sentence types, in either natural or inverted order, may be used. Answers will vary.

Page 120
Affirm quality:
Ascertain all the distinguishing properties.
Affirm class or kind:
These exercises are similar to the one on page **119**. Answer will vary.

Page 122
168. EXERCISE IN ANALYSIS.

All sentences in this exercise are delcarative and simple. All but numbers **10, 13,** and **14** begin with the subject, followed by an action verb as predicate. The subject in **10** and **13** is **you**, understood, and **you** is the subject of **14**.

In sentences **1-9**, and **11**, the final word in the sentence is the direct object, which receives the action of the verb.

Sentences **10, 12, 13,** and **15-20** have indirect objects which may be identified from the direct objects by changing them to prepositional phrases. These are: **10. (to) me; (12. (for) director; 13. (to) him; 15. (to) me; 17. (to) Eli; 18. (for) monitor; 19. (for) day; 20. (for) leader.**

The direct objects in the remaining sentences are: **10. music; 12. him; 13. book; 14. whom; 15. horse; 16. algebra; 17. velocipede; John; 19. light; 20. him; Their** in **20** is a possessive pronoun functioning as an adjective modifying **leader**.

169. EXERCISES IN SYNTHESES

These exercises require the student to use direct and indirect objects, using subjects and verbs supplied by the text. Remind the students that indirect objects may be changed to prepositional phrases, usually beginning with **to** or **for**. Though the indirect object usually preceeds the direct object, this is not always the case.

Page 124
172. EXERCISES IN ANALYSIS

All senences in this exercise are declarative and simple.

1. House, subject; **was burned**, predicate. **A** and **large**, adjectives, modify the subject, **house**.

2. I, subject; **wrote**, predicate. **A** and **long**, adjectives, modify **letter**, the direct object of **wrote**.

3. Land, subject; **property**, predicate; **is**, copula. **This**, an adjective, modifies the subject **land**; and the adjective **government** modifies the predicate noun **property**.

4. Hands, subject; **make**, predicate; **work**, object. **Many** and **quick** are adjectives modifying **hands** and **work**, respectively.

5. Son, subject; **maketh**, predicate; **father**, object. **And** and **wise** are adjectives modifying **son**; **a** and **glad** modify **father**.

6. Necessity, subject; **opportunity**, predicate; **is**, copula. **Man's**, adjective, modifies **necessity**; **God's**, adjective, modifies the predicate.

7. Mr. Hodge, subject; **hired**, predicate; **Mr. Olds**, object. **Farmer**, noun in apposition, functions as an adjective to modify **Mr. Hodge**; and **mason**, a noun in apposition, functions adjectively to modify **Mr. Olds**. **The**, an adjective used twice, modifies **farmer** and **mason**, respectively.

8. Mary, subject; **has chosen**, predicate; **part**, object. **The** and **better**, adjectives, modify **part**.

9. Barking, subject; **wakened**, predicate; **family**, object. **Carlo's**, a possessive noun, is used as an adjective to modify **barking**. **The**, adjective, modifies **family**.

10. I, subject; **saw**, predicate; **swans**, object. **Six**, adjective, modifies **swans**.

11. **This**, subject; **birthday**, predicate; **is**, copula. **My** and **fourteenth** are adjectives modifying the predicate noun **birthday**.

12. **Man**, subject; **received**, predicate; **penny**, object. **Every**, adjective, modifies **man**; and **a**, an adjective, modifies **penny**.

173. EXERCISES IN SYNTHESIS

Students should compose their own sentences, using the words suggested on these pages as adjectives or nouns, as required. After the teacher has checked their work, they should analyze their sentences, as in 172.

Page 125
176. EXERCISES IN ANALYSIS

All sentences in this exercise are declarative and simple.

1. **Birds**, subject; **sing**, predicate, modified by **sweetly**, an adverb. **The**, adjective, modifies the subject, **birds**.

2. **We**, subject; **struck**, predicate; **vessel**, object, modified by **the**, an adjective. **Amidships**, adverb, modifies **struck**; and **just**, adverb, modifies **amidships**.

3. **I**, subject; **require**, predicate; **votes**, object. **Now**, adverb, modifies the verb **require**; and **your**, possessive of **you**, is used as an adjective modifying the noun **votes**.

4. **He**, subject; **lived**, predicate. **Formerly** and **here**, adverbs, modify the verb **lived**.

5. **Fire**, subject; **went**, predicate. **The**, adjective, modifies **fire**; and **out**, adverb, modifies **went**.

6. **He**, subject; **sad**, predicate, modified by **very**, adverb. **Seems** is the copula. **Sad**, predicate adjective, modifies the subject, **he**.

7. **Boy**, subject; **wrote**, predicate; **letter**, object. **The** is an adjective in both uses. It modifies **boy** or **letter**. **Carelesssly**, adverb, modifies the verb **wrote**.

8. **They**, subject; **absent**, predicate (predicate adjective); **long**, adverb modifying **absent**; **have been**, copula.

9. **I**, subject; **shall defend**, predicate; **you**, object. **Certainly**, a modal adverb, modifies the entire clause.

Page 128
181. EXERCISES

All the sentences in this exercise are declarative and simple.

1. **Thou**, subject; **hast uttered**, predicate; **words**, object; **cruel**, adjective, modifies **words**.

2. **Heart**, subject; **knows**, predicate; **sorrows**, object. **Every**, adjective, modifies **heart**; and **its**, adjective, modifies **sorrows**.

3. **Gratitude**, subject; **emotion**, a predicate noun, is the predicate; **is**, copula. **A** and **delightful**, adjectives, modify **emotion**.

4. **Bounty**, subject; **was bestowed**, predicate, modified by **well**, an adverb. **This** and **generous**, adjectives, modify **bounty**.

5. **Men**, subject; **experience**, predicate; **disappointments**, object. **The** and **best**, adjectives, modify **men**; **often**, adverb, modifies the verb **experience**.

6. **Disposition**, subject; **will secure**, predicate; **regard**, object. **A** and **amiable**, adjectives, modify **disposition**; and **universal**, an adjective, modifies **regard**. **So**, adverb, modifies **amiable**.

7. **Offence**, subject; **will condemn**, predicate; **him**, object. **His** and **brother's** are used as adjectives to modify the subject, **offence**. **Not**, adverb, modifies the verb **will condemn**.

183. EXERCISES

All the sentences in this exercise are declarative and simple.

1. **Crags**, subject; **pierce**, predicate; **sky**, object. **Black**, and **behind thee**, a prepositional phrase, are adjectives modifying **crags**. **The**, **clear**, and **blue**, adjectives, modify **sky**.

2. **Vicissitudes**, subject; **fill**, predicate; **life**, object. **Of good and evil**, adjective, modifies **vicissitudes**; **the** and **of man**, adjectives, modify **life**; and **up**, adverb, modifies the verb **fill**.

3. **He**, subject; **had**, predicate; **view**, object. **A** and **good**, adjectives, modify **view**, a noun. **Remarkably**, adverb, modifies **good**; and **of their features**, adjective, modifies **view**.

4. **He**, subject; **shakes**, predicate; **woods**, object. **The**, and **on the mountain side**, adjectives modifying **woods**.

5. **Fate**, subject; **thine**, predicate; **may be**, copula, modified by **well**, an adverb. **The** and **of the gods** are adjectives modifying **fate**. **Thine**, possessive of **thy** is here equivalent to **thy fate**. Its antecedent is **fate**. **Thine** is here a predicate noun.

6. **He**, subject; **had endured**, predicate; **months**, object. **Three** and **of nights** are adjectives modifying **months**.

7. **Architecture**, subject; **framework**, a predicate noun, is the predicate; **had become**, copula. **His**, adjective, modifies **architecture**. **A**, **mere**, and **for the setting**, adjectives, modify **framework**; and **of delicate sculpture**, adjective prepositional phrase, modifies **setting**.

Page 129
185. EXERCISES.

1. **I**, subject; **bow**, predicate. **Reverently** and **to**

decrees are adverbs modifying **bow**. **Thy**, adjective, modifies **decrees**.

2. **Heaven**, subject; **burns**, predicate; **with sun**, adverb phrase, modifies **burns**; **the** and **descending**, adjectives, modify **sun**.

3. **Track**, subject; **fresh**, predicate; **is**, copula. **The** and **panther's**, adjectives, modify **track**. **In snow**, adverb phrase, modifies the predicate adjective, **fresh**, which in turn modifies **track**. **The**, adjective, modifies **snow**.

4. **Home**, subject; **lay**, predicate. **His**, adjective, modifies **home**. **Low** and **in the valley**, adverbs, modify the verb **lay**.

5. **We**, subject; **descried**, predicate; **object**, direct object. **Day** is a noun in the objective case without a governing word (cf. p.157, Rule VIII). It may be perceived as the object of **of** in the elliptical prepositional phrase, **of one day**, an adverbial phrase modifying **descried**. **One**, adjective, modifies **day**.

Some, **shapeless**, and **floating**, adjectives, modify **object**. **At a distance** is an adverbial phrase modifying the participle adjective **floating**.

6. **Horses**, subject; **ran**, predicate. **Miles**, noun in the objective case without a governing word, functions as an adverbial phrase equal to **of miles**, modifying **ran**. **Two**, adjective, modifies the noun **miles**. **Without stopping**, adverbial phrase, modifies **ran**.

7. **We**, subject; **sailed**, predicate. **South** and **days** are objective nouns without governing words (prepositions), equal to the adverbial prepositional phrases **toward the south** and **for days**, both modifying the verb **sailed**. **Four**, adjective, modifies **days**.

8. **You**, understood, subject; **see**, predicate. **What ... brow**, relative clause, is the object of the verb **see**. **What** is a definitive adjective limiting **grace**, also modified by **a**. **Grace** is the subject of the relative noun clause; **is seated**, its predicate. **On brow**, adverbial phrase, modifies **is seated**; and **his**, adjective, modifies **brow**.

9. **There** is here the anticipatory subject, used idiomatically; **life**, predicate noun, is the predicate; **is**, copula. **A** and **very**, adjectives, modify **life**. **In despair**, adverbial phrase modifying the copula, **is**. **Our**, adjective, modifies **life**.

10. **Sunshine**, subject; **settles**, predicate. **Eternal**, adjective, modifies **sunshine**; **on head**, adverb phrase, modifies the verb **settles**; **his**, adjective, modifies **head**.

11. **Heaven**, subject; **taught**, predicate; **letters**, object. **First** and **for aid**, adverbial elements modifying **taught**. **Wretch's**, adjective, modifies **aid**; and **some**, adverb, modifies **wretch's**.

187. EXERCISES

All the sentences in this exercise are declarative and simple.

Here are the functions of the infinitives in this exercise:

1. **To doubt**, subject; **promise** is its object.

2. The infinitive **to write** and the prepositional phrase, **to his office**, both function adverbially to modify **has gone**. **Letter** is the object of **to write**.

3. **To see** is the predicate noun; functions to modify the idiomatic subject **it**; **sun**, object of **to see**.

4. **To know**, subject; **me** is the object of **to know**.

5. **To command** is the predicate noun; functions to modify the idiomatic subject **it**, which is contained in the contraction, **'tis**. **Success** is the object of **command**.

6. **To soothe**, adjective, modifies **charms**. **Breast** is its object.

7. **To venture**, adverb, modifies **enough**. **Quarrel** is the object of **to venture**.

8. **To found**, adverb, modifies **serve**. **State** is the object of **to found**.

Pages 130-131
189. EXERCISES

All the sentences in this exercise are declarative and complex except number **7**, which is simple and declarative, and number **13**, which is exclamatory and complex.

Here are shortened answers, showing the relationships of the clauses of each sentence. The teacher may wish to have the students also identify the relationships of individual words, as shown in the sample of complete analysis on page **130**.

1. **Those soon rested** is the main clause. **Who fought**, the relative clause, is an adjective element modifying **those**, subject of the verb, **rested**.

2. **All said** is the main clause; **that Love had suffered wrong** is the subordinate clause, which functions as a noun, object of the verb **said**. **That**, subordinate conjunction, introduces the clause.

3. **He builds** is the main clause, modified by the adverbial clause **where the torrents fall**, introduced by the conjunctive adverb **where**.

4. **It was**, main clause. **Now**, adverb, modifies the copula, **was**; **matter** is the predicate noun, modified by the adjective prepositional phrase, **of curiosity**. **Who the old gentleman was**, a relative clause, like the phrase, is used adjectively to modify **matter**.

5. **Fires complete** is the main clause. **What the fires have not consumed**, the dependent noun clause, is the object of the verb **complete** in the main

clause, to which it is joined by the conjunctive pronoun, **what**.

6. The schoolmaster walked is the main clause. **Walked**, the verb, is modified adverbially by **over to the cottage**, an adverbial prepositional phrase, and by **where his little friend lay sick**, an adverb clause, introduced by the conjunctive adverb **where**. (*Or*, **where . . . lay sick** may be treated as an adjective clause modifying **cottage**. **Where** is a conjunctive adverb in either case.)

7. Sound, subject; **sound** (second use) predicate noun; **was**, copula. **Longer**, adverb, modifies the copula, **was. No**, adverb, modifies **longer**.

8. These are, main clause; **follies** is the predicate noun. **On which it would be folly**, adjective relative clause, modifies **follies**. It is joined to the main clause by the conjunctive prepositional phrase, **on which**, in which **which** functions both as a relative pronoun and the object of the preposition, **on**.

9. I am, main clause, modified adverbially by the prepositional phrase **at liberty** and the infinitive **to confess**. All which follows is a noun clause, the direct object of **to confess**, to which it is joined by the conjunctive pronoun **that**.

Much, an indefinite noun, is the subject of this objective noun clause; its verb is **was founded**, modified by **well. Which I have heard objected to** is an adjective clause within the noun clause, introduced by the phrase, **to which. I** is the subject and **have heard objected** is its verb. This adjective clause modifies the noun, **much**.

(In) my late friend's writing is an adverb phrase with a gerund object, modifying **have heard objected**.

10. One, subject of the main clause; its verb is the copula **was. Of . . . maxims**, an adjective prepositional phrase, modifies **one**. The entire remainder of this sentence, **was . . . one**, is a complex noun clause serving as the predicate noun and modifying **one**.

That, conjunction, introduces the noun clause; **is**, its copula. **To keep** and **to let**, infinitives, modify **way. Anyone**, the object of **to let**, is modified by the infinitive, **(to) suspect**, which has as its object the noun clause **you have one**, introduced by **that**.

11. How his essays will read now that they are brought together is a complex noun clause, functioning as the subject of the verb **is**, its copula. Within this complex clause, **essays** is the subject of the chief secondary clause; **will read** is the verb. **Now . . . together**, adjective clause, modifies **essays**. Its subject is **they**; **are brought** is the verb.

Question, predicate noun, modifies all that preceeds the copula, **is. For the publishers**, an adjective prepositional phrase, modifies **question**.

Who, a relative pronoun, is the subject of a second adjective clause, which modifies **publishers**. Its verb is **have ventured**.

To draw, infinitive, adverbially modifies **have ventured**; **to draw** is modified in turn by **out**, an adverb, and **into one piece**, a prepositional phrase.

Follies, a noun, is the object of **to draw**. It is modified by **his** and the participle, **weaved-up**.

12. The first line of this verse is the main clause of this compound-complex sentence. **You**, understood, is the subject; **sing** is the verb. **Wind**, a noun in the absolute case, is the antecedent of **you**.

For . . . tonight, subordinate clause, modifies the main clause. **There** is the subject; **is** the copula; **music**, the predicate noun. **Made**, a participle, modifies **music**.

That . . . hear, an adjective clause, also modifies **music. I** is its subject; **would hear**, the verb. **Fain**, an adverb meaning **gladly**, modifies the verb.

13. Woe is the subject of both these exclamatory clauses in this line of poetry. **Worth**, here the copula, is an archaic verb form of **to be. Chase** and **day** are predicate nouns.

That, a relative pronoun, is the subject of the relative adjective clause, **that . . . life**, modifying both **chase** and **day** in the first line. **Cost** is its verb, and **life**, the object. **Gray**, a noun of direct address, is in the absolute case.

(Students may find number **13** difficult because of the archaic use of **worth** and their perception of **woe** as an interjection. Don't let them give up until they first consult a good unabridged or collegiate dictionary, however.)

14. Mountain is the subject of the main clause; **arose**, the verb. **Shadow**, subject of the adverbial subordinate clause; **was sleeping**, the verb.

Page 132
193. EXERCISES

All the sentences in this exercise are declarative and simple. All begin with the noun or pronoun grammatical subject, or an infinitive functioning as the grammatical subject.

1. Banners, grammatical subject; **were waving** is the grammatical predicate.

2. To forgive, grammatical subject; **divine**, grammatical predicate; **is**, copula.

3. It, grammatical subject; **pleasant**, grammatical predicate; **is**, copula. **Pleasant** is modified by the adverbial infinitive, **to read**.

(*Note:* **To read is pleasant** *says about the same thing without employing the idiomatic* **it**. *This merely shifts the emphasis from* **pleasant**, *an adjective, to* **to read**, *an infinitive, which in this use becomes a noun.*)

4. **Stars**, grammatical subject; **have been shining**, grammatical predicate.

5. **Weapons**, grammatical subject; **were procured**, grammatical predicate.

6. **To covet**, grammatical subject; **sinful**, grammatical predicate; **is**, copula.

7. **To quarrel**, grammatical subject; **disgraceful**, grammatical predicate; **is**, copula.

8. **To rob**, grammatical subject; **to plunder**, grammatical predicate; **is**, copula.

9. **Vessels**, grammatical subject; **are**, grammatical predicate. **Are** is modified by the prepositional phrase **in sight**, an adverbial element.

Page 135
196. EXERCISES

Here are shortened answers, showing the relation between complex elements. The teacher may wish to have students work out one or two of these in full for practice.

1. This sentence is declarative, complex. **Limit**, the grammatical predicate is modified by the adjective clause **forbearance ceases**, which is introduced by the adjective phrase, **at which**. **To be a virtue**, infinitive phrase, modifies **ceases**.

There is both the simple and the complete subject. The remainder of the sentence is the complete predicate.

2. This sentence is declarative, complex. **If**, conjunction, introduces the adverbial clause, **ye love me**, which modifies the main clause, **(you) keep my commandments**.

You, understood, is both the simple and the complete subject; all the remainder is the complete predicate.

Sentences **3**, **4**, and **5**, like **2**, are inverted complex sentences with one-word complete subjects, and the remainder of the words consisting of the complete predicate.

3. This sentence is declarative, complex. **Were I Alexander** is equivalent to **if I were Alexander**, an adverbial clause modifying the main clause, **I would be Diogenes**, in this inverted sentence.

4. This sentence is declarative, complex. **Unless**, conjunction, introduces the adverbial clause, **he reforms soon**, which modifies the main clause, **he is a ruined man**.

5. This sentence is declarative, complex. **Except**, adverbial conjunction, joins the subordinate clause, **ye repent**, to the main clause, **ye shall all likewise perish**, which it modifies.

6. This sentence is declarative, complex. **You**, understood, is both the simple and complete subject; **withdraw . . . thee** is the complete predicate.

Lest, conjunction, introduces the adverbial clause, **he weary of thee, and so hate thee**, modifying the main clause, **(you) withdraw thy foot from thy neighbor's house**.

7. This sentence is declarative, complex. **I** is both the simple and the complete subject. **Am**, copula; **quite . . . morning**, complete predicate.

Sure, a modal adverb modifying the main clause, **I am**, is itself modified by the adverb **quite**, and also by the adverbial clause, **Mr. Hutchins . . . morning**, introduced by the conjunction, **that**.

8. This sentence is declarative, complex. **He** is the subject of the main clause; **never . . . study** is the complete predicate. **He is too lazy to study**, subordinate clause, adverbially modifies the verb of the main clause, **knows**, to which it is joined by **because**, a conjunction.

9. This sentence is declarative, complex. **You**, understood, is the subject of the main clause; **do not forget to write when you reach home**, complete predicate. **Do forget**, the simple predicate, is modified by **to write**, an infinitive, by **not**, an adverb, and by **you reach home**, adverb clause, introduced by the adverb, **when**.

10. This sentence is declarative, simple, consisting of **we**, subject, and its complete predicate, the remainder of the sentence. **Belong**, the verb, is modified by the adverb **even**, and the adverbial phrases **by means** and **to the eternal plan**. **Of our sorrows**, an adjective phrase, modifies **means**, object of the preposition **by**.

11. This sentence is declarative, complex. **Gentleman** is the simple subject; **had**, the simple predicate, **The . . . black** constitutes the complete subject, which is the simple subject with its modifiers. **Had . . . man** is the complete predicate.

Who was dressed in brown-once-black, adjective clause, modifies **gentleman**. **Sort**, a noun, the object of **had**, is modified by the phrase **of exterior**, in turn modified by the adjective clause, **which . . . man**.

12. This sentence is declarative, simple. **Art**, simple subject; **was practiced**, simple predicate, modified by the adverbial infinitive phrase **to make**. **Them**, object of **to make** is modified in turn by the participle, **pleased**, in turn modified by the adverbial phrase **with condition**.

13. This sentence is declarative, complex. **Man**, simple subject; **brute**, predicate noun; **is**, copula. **That**, pronoun, is the subject of the adjective clause, **that blushes**, modifying **man**. **Blushes** is the verb of the clause. **Not**, an adverb, modifies the copula, **is**. **Quite**, a modal adverb, modifies the main clause, **The man is a brute**.

14. This sentence is declarative, complex. **Soul**, simple subject; **boat**, predicate noun; **is**, copula.

Which . . . float, adjective clause, modifies **boat**. **Like . . . swan**, adverbial prepositional phrase, modifies **float**; **upon waves**, adverbial phrase, modifies **float**; and **of singing**, adjective phrase, modifies **waves**.

Page 137
199. EXERCISES

1. **Exercise and tempermant** is the compound subject; **strengthen**, the predicate; **constitution**, its object.

2. **Youth** is the subject; **bright and lovely**, the compound predicate adjective; **is**, the copula.

3. **He** is the subject; **old nor infirm**, compound predicate adjective, modified by **neither**; **is**, the copula.

4. **He** is the subject; **angry, but excited**, the compound predicate adjective; **is**, the copula, modified by **not**, an adverb.

5. **They**, subject; **wash, iron, cook, eat, and sleep**, is the compound simple predicate. **In the same room**, an adverbial prepositional phrase, modifies the predicate.

6. **I**, subject; **want**, simple predicate. **To be quiet and be let alone**, infinitive phrases, are compound adverbial elements modifying the verb **want**.

7. **Book**, simple subject; **present**, predicate noun; **was**, copula. **Which I loaned you, and which you lost** are compound adjective elements (two clauses joined by the conjunction **and**) which modify **book**.

8. **To live and (to) drive** is a compound infinitive phrase used as a noun subject; **height**, predicate noun; **is**, copula.

9. **There**, subject; **tap**, predicate noun; **was**, copula. **Tap** (second use) is a noun in apposition to **tap** (first use), modified by the adjectives **a, smart**, and **potential**, and by the adjective clause, **which seemed**. **To say**, an infinitive, modifies the verb **seemed**. "**Here I am and in I'm coming,**" clauses, are the compound object of **to say**.

10. This is a declarative compound sentence consisting of three main clauses, **not . . . given, brows . . . it**, and **souls . . . striven**, joined by the conjunctions **but** and **and**. **Truth** is the subject of the first clause; **has been given**, the simple predicate. **To art or to science**, a compound prepositional phrase joined by the conjunction **or**, modifies **has been given**. **Brows** is the subject of the second clause; **have ached**, the simple predicate. **Souls** is the subject of the third clause; **toiled and striven**, the compound predicate.

Page 139
202. EXERCISES
Classify the phrases and clauses:

1. **To his assistance**—prepositional phrase, adverbial.

2. **Were not Romans hinds = if Romans were not hinds**—adverbial clause, conditional.

3. **That ye all spake**—objective clause. **With tongues**—prepositional phrase, adverbial.

4. **As thyself**—prepositional phrase, adverbial.

5. (Contains no phrase or clause.)

6. **(To) give**—infinitive phrase, adverbial.

7. **That you may meet them**—adverbial clause, final.

8. **Who might have seen him**—relative clause, adjective. **Of his majestic stature**—prepositional phrase, adverbial.

9. **A mighty people**—appositive phrase. **For the regeneration**—prepositional phrase, adverbial. **Of Europe**—prepositional phrase, adjective.

10. **Not many generations ago**—adverbial phrase. **Where you now sit circled**—adverbial clause, local. **With all**—prepositional phrase, adverbial. **That exalts and embellishes civilized life**—relative clause, adjective, modifies **all**.

11. **Properly speaking**—participial phrase, adverbial. **At present**—prepositional phrase, adverbial. **At present**—prepositional phrase, adverbial. **To live another time**—infinitive phrase, adverbial.

12. **In numbers**—prepositional phrase, adverbial. **For the numbers came**—adverbial clause, causal.

13. **While the bridegroom tarried**—adverbial clause, temporal.

14. **Whose laws and phenomena**—relative clause, adjective.

15. **Since they are known** and **because they exist**—adverbial clauses, both causal.

16. **At ten o'clock**—prepositional phrase, adverbial. **My task being finished**—absolute phrase, adverbial. **To the river**—prepositional phrase, adverbial.

17. The subject of the first clause of this complex, declarative sentence is **some**; **say**, the simple predicate. The three lines which follow (**that . . . long**) comprise a complex objective clause, the object of the verb **say**. **That**, a conjunction, introduces this clause. The clauses and phrases within it are here identified and their relationships noted:

Ever gainst that season comes = before and against (in preparation of) **the coming of that season**—complex adverbial phrase modifying **singeth**.

Wherein our Savior's birth is celebrated—relative clause modifying **season**.

This bird singeth—objective clause, object of **say**.

Of warning—prepositional phrase, adjective.

All night long—adverbial phrase modifying **singeth**.

No spirit dares stir, the nights are wholesome, no planets strike, and no tales nor witch hath power—main clause, parallel to **some say**.

To charm—infinitive phrase, adjective, modifying **power**.

(Because) so hallowed and so gracious is the time—adverbial clause modifying all clauses preceeding, beginning with **no spirit dares stir**.

Page 141
205. EXERCISES

Here are the contracted, elliptical sentences expanded with the words necessary to show the relationships among the elements. You may wish to have your students analyze them fully, following the samples on pages 140-141.

1. (You) **advance**.
2. (You get) **up, comrades,** (you get) **up**.
3. (You be) **quick, or we are lost**. (Only **to be** or another linking verb will do for the verb here, since **quick** is an adjective. **Quickly**, however, would require a transitive verb.)
4. (Is this/are you) **honest, my lord?**
5. (That/this is) **impossible!**
6. **This** (having been) **done, we instantly departed**.
7. (Art) **thou denied a grave!**
8. **What would content you?** (Would) **talent** (content you)?
9. **How, now Jenkinson,** (does that affect you)? (Any of many clauses could be supplied here to give the adverbs **how** and **now** a verb [eg. **does affect**] to modify. **Jenkinson**, in any case, is absolute.)
10. (You throw) **a rope to the side!**
11. **Rather he** (die/go, etc).
12. (He was) **the orphan of St. Louis,** (and) **he** . . .
13. **Do you see a man** (who is) **wise** . . . ?
14. . . . (I am) **somewhat** (fond of skating).
15. **Horace is older than I** (am old)?
16. **That building is as large as the capitol** (is large).
17. **Ere we who saw** (them) **were conscious of** (their) **change, multitudes of little floating clouds** (had) **pierced through their ethereal texture,** (and they) **had become** (as) **vivid as fire**.
18. **Then here's** (a toast) **to our boyhood,** (to) **its gold and** (to) **its gray,** (to) **the stars of its winter** (and to) **the dews of its May! And when we have done** (playing) **with our life-lasting toys,** (we pray to thee,) **dear Father,** (You) **take care of Thy children,** (known as) **the Boys!**

19-25. (No ellipses.)

26. (You) **learn to labor and to wait**.

27-31. (No ellipses.)

Pages 144-145
208. EXERCISES

Here follows the expansions of these abridged propositions. Students should also analyze a few of them for practice, following the models on page 144.

1. (Since) **Caesar crossed the Rubicon, Pompey prepared for battle**.
2. (Since) **he had accumulated** . . . .
3. (Since) **you be but dust, you be humble and wise**.
4. **I should judge from his dress, and** (therefore) **I should pronounce him to be an artisan**.
5. **I believe that he is an honest man**.
6. **There is no hope that he will recover his health**.
7. **There is no prospect that the storm will abate**.
8. **He was detained by this accident,** (and so) **he lost the opportunity of seeing them**.
9. **They annoyed us thus for a time,** (and then) **they began to form themselves into close columns, six or eight** (standing) **abreast**.
10. (When) **my story was done, she gave me for my pains a world of sighs**.

Page 147-149
212. MISCELLANEOUS EXAMPLES

These practice exercises may be used with the "Model for complete analysis" (number 210), or for any make-up work the teacher may deem the student needs.

Page 151
213. SUBJECT-NOMINATIVE

To be corrected, analyzed, and parsed. Corrections follow. Analysis and parsing may be done, if needed, by rules found earlier in the text.

1. **He and I study grammar**.
2. **those horses** (are)
3. **John and I**
4. **Who besides me?** (Who got a prize besides me?)
5. **I am as tall as he** (is tall), **but she is taller than he** (is tall).
6. **Who has come**
7. **he** (is) **but naked though** (he be) **locked**
8. **I do** (want an orange).
9. **as she** (is studious)

PAGE 151-155

10. **I** (am old)
11. **who else are expected**
12. **None . . . is more beloved than he** (is beloved).

Page 152
EXERCISES
To be corrected, analyzed, and parsed:
1. It is **I**.
2. It was **she** and **he** whom you saw (**you saw whom**—objective case).
3. If I were **he**
4. **Who**
5. **Who** (They are who)
6. It was not **I** nor **he** who
7. It is not **they** who
8. **they.** (**They** is here the predicate nominative in the participial phrase, **its being they**. But since this phrase is used as the object of **of, they** has a strained sound to many speakers. **No doubt they are the ones** avoids this difficulty.)

215. POSSESSIVE CASE
   1. **boy's** or **boys'**
   2. of the **Knights templars**
   3. the **Merchant's** Union Express
   4. **his**
   5. The **Bishop of Dublin's**
   6. **father's**
   7. **yours**
   8. the **teacher's**, not the pupil's
   9. The horse of the **general's aide** was killed.
  10. **his**
  11. **Penfields', the bookseller** (This is not a compound because of the comma after **Penfields'** and no cap on **bookseller. Bookseller** is in apposition to **Penfields'**.)
  12. the beheading of **France's King Louis XVI,** *or* the beheading of **Louis XVI, King of France**
  13. **William and Mary's** (They were joint sovereigns.)
  14. It was **John's** fault, not **Emma's**.

Pages 153-154
216. APPOSITION
To be corrected, analyzed, and parsed:
1. **Will you desert me—me who have**
2. **he**
3. of Mrs. Wilson; **her**
4. **he**
5. **them**
6. **Wilkins the blacksmith's**
7. **They are the lovely, they**

217. NOMINATIVE ABSOLUTE CASE
EXERCISES
Examples to be parsed. In these nine examples, we have supplied the ellipses where they seem to fit without being awkward, and have identified the other nouns as nominative absolute, Rule V.
  1. **Soldier, (thou mayest) rest! Thy warfare (is) o'er. Soldier** is a noun, nominative absolute, Rule V.
  2. **"(You) stop!" Hat**—noun, nominative absolute, Rule V.
  3. **Where are our fathers?**
  4. **Since I was a child, this was . . . .**
  5. **Thou hast created the north and the south.**
  6. **John, James, and Henry are my scholars.**
  7. **Nelly Gray** is a noun, nominative absolute, Rule V.
  8. **"The Moon and the Stars—A Fable"** is a compound proper noun. Since we do not know how this title—of whatever—is used, it is impossible to construct an ellipsis. It is a noun, nominative, absolute, Rule V.
  9. **Here is Problem III—To construct a mean proportional between two given lines.**

Pages 154-155
218. OBJECTIVE CASE
EXERCISES
Examples to be corrected:
  1. **Whom did you write to?** (to whom)
  2. . . .let **him** and (let) **me** . . . .
  3. I do not know **whom** to trust.
  4. **Him** . . . , not **me** (Punish him; do not punish me.)
  5. I saw **her** and **him** . . . .
  6. And **I**, what shall I do? (I is appositive to I.)
  7. . . . **he** and **I** (will go) (appositive to **we**.)
  8. . . . but **him** . . . .
  9. (Correct)
 10. (for) **whom** . . . ?

Examples to be analyzed and parsed (parsing has been abbreviated):
  1. **Homes**—noun, objective case, object of **will build**, Rule VI.
  2. **Lips**—noun, objective case, object of **shall pass**.
  3. **That at sea all is vacancy**—noun clause, objective case, object of **have left**, Rule VI.
  4. **What there they found**—noun clause, objective case, object of **have left**, Rule VI.
  5. **Model**—noun, objective case, object of **bring**, Rule VI.
  6. **Him**—pronoun, objective case, object of **fires**, Rule VI.

7. **Man** (all three uses)—noun, objective case, object of **makes**, Rule VI.

8. **Son**—noun, objective case, object of **hast left**, Rule VI.

9. **Who, then, can be saved?**—noun clause, objective case, object of **said**, Rule VI.

10. **"But what good came of it at last?"**—noun clause, objective case, object of **quoth**, Rule VI. **"Why, that I cannot tell,"** and **"But 'twas a famous victory"**—both noun clauses, objective case, object of **said**, Rule VI.

Pages 156-157
219. OBJECTIVE AFTER PREPOSITIONS
EXERCISES
To be corrected:
1. **The army shall not want supplies.**
2. **To which school . . . ?**
3. **For what firm . . . ?**
4. **Of what country . . . ?**
5. **I will not permit such conduct.**
6. **It is our duty to assist those in distress and to sympathize with them.**
7. **The convicts are hired by a few speculators, for which they are employed.**
8. **He lives in Pittsburg and he came from there,** or, **he lives in Pittsburg from whence he came.**

Page 157
To be analyzed and parsed. Here follows abbreviated analyses of these exercise sentences; note that the adjectives have been left out of the phrases to clarify the relationship between the nouns and the prepositions.

1. **For hours** and **in fog**, both adverbial prepositional phrases, modify **cruised**, a verb. **Hours** and **fog**, nouns, are the objects of **for** and **in**, Rule VII.

2. **Upon lap**, adverbial prepositional phrase, modifies **rests**, a verb. **Of earth**, adjective prepositional phrase, modifies **lap**. **Lap** and **earth**, are the objects of **upon**, Rule VII.

3. **Out of cloister**, compound adverbial prepositional phrase, modifies **will steal**, a verb. **Cloister**, a noun, is the object of the compound preposition, **out of**, Rule VII.

4. **Into earth**, adverbial prepositional phrase, modifies **sank**, a verb. **Earth**, a noun, is the object of the preposition, **into**, Rule VII.

5. **Like sea**, adverbial prepositional phrase, modifies **lifts**, a verb. **Sea**, a noun, is the object of the preposition, **like**, Rule VII.

6. **In sky** and **like squadrons**, adverbial prepositional phrases, modify **are driven**, a verb, which is also modified by the adverb **about**. **Sky** and **squadrons**, nouns, are the objects of the prepositions, **in** and **like**, Rule VII.

Of combatants, an adjective prepositional phrase, modifies the noun **squadrons**. **Combatants**, a noun, is the object of the preposition, **of**, Rule VII.

To conflict, adverbial prepositional phrase, modifies the participle **rushing**, which in turn adjectively modifies **combatants**. **Conflict**, noun, is the object of **to**, a preposition, Rule VII.

7. **In vain**, adverbial prepositional phrase, modifies the verb **does rage**. **Vain**, an adjective parsed as a noun, is the object of **in**, a preposition, Rule VII.

8. **Till lately**, adverbial prepositional phrase, modifies the verb, **had supposed**. **Lately**, an adverb parsed as a noun, is the object of the preposition, **till**, Rule VII.

9. **Round the globe**, adverbial prepositional phrase, modifies the verb **tumbled**. **Globe**, a noun, is the object of the preposition, **round**, Rule VII.

10. **Without sun**, adverbial prepositional phrase, modifies the verb **broke**. **Sun**, a noun, is the object of the preposition, **without**, Rule VII.

Pages 157-158
To be analyzed and parsed:

Mile (1.), **straw** (2.), **dollars** (3.), **years** (4.), **cloak-fashion** (5.), **times** (6.), **four knots**, and **hour** (7.), are all nouns in the objective case without a governing word, functioning as adverbial prepositional phrases modifying the verbs **ran**, **do care**, the adjective **worth**, and the verbs **is**, **wore**, **has covered**, and **sailed**, Rule VIII.

8. **Remembering**, a participle noun (gerund), functions as an adverbial phrase to modify the adjective **worth**, Rule VIII.

9. **Feet**, a noun, functions as a predicate adjective phrase to modify **tower**, Rule VIII.

10. **Feet**, a noun in the objective case without a governing word (all three uses), adjectively modifies **room**. **Feet**, in turn, is modified adjectively by **twenty-one**, **fifteen**, **ten**, **long**, **wide**, and **high**; Rule VIII.

11. **Diploma**, a noun in the objective case without a governing word, adverbially modifies **was refused**, Rule VIII.

Page 159
EXERCISES
To be corrected:
1. **James has been whispering.**
2. **Whom when they had washed, they laid** (omit the first comma—**they had washed whom**). This quote is from Acts 9:37. The antecedent of **whom** is **Tabitha** (cf. v. 36).

3. I am sorry for the names I called you.
4. If anyone . . . his fare, let him call . . . .
5. Everyone should have his life insured.
6. . . . his life . . . .
7. That book, which contains pictures, is in the bookcase, or, That picture book is in the bookcase.
8. This is the dog which . . . .
9. (Were men captured? Guns? Both? Did the men help capture the guns? The student must rewrite to show which.)
10. That is the same pen I sold you.
11. . . . who . . . .
12. (Correct), **or, her station still higher**
13. their
14. the messengers or it
15. of it

Page 160

To be parsed:

1. **That**—pronoun, relative, its antecedent is **hand**; simple, neuter, third person, singular, Rule IX; nominative, Rule I.

2. **I** (both uses)—pronoun, personal, its antecedent is the name, understood, of the speaker; gender unknown, first person, singular, Rule IX; nominative, Rule I.

Which—pronoun, relative, its antecedent is **people**; simple, common gender, third person, plural, Rule IX; third person, plural, Rule IX; objective, object of **made**, Rule VI.

3. **Him**—pronoun, personal, simple, its antecedent is the name, understood, of the person spoken of; masculine, third person, singular, Rule IX; objective, Rule VI.

Who—pronoun, relative, its antecedent is **him**, masculine, third person, singular, Rule IX; nominative, Rule I.

4. **I**—pronoun, personal, simple, its antecedent is the name, understood, of the speaker; gender unknown, first person, singular, Rule IX; nominative, Rule I.

Whose—pronoun, relative, its antecedent is **man**; masculine, third person, singular, Rule IX; possessive, modifies **heart**, Rule III.

5. **Your**—pronoun, personal, simple, its antecedent is the name, understood, of the person spoken to; gender unknown, second person, number unknown, Rule IX; possessive, Rule III.

Our—pronoun, personal, simple, its antecedent is the name, understood, of the speakers; common gender, first person, plural, Rule IX; possessive, Rule III.

6. **Her**—pronoun, personal, simple, its antecedent is the name, understood, of the person spoken of; feminine, third person, singular, Rule IX; possessive, Rule III.

7. **That** (both uses)—pronoun, relative, its antecedent is **birds** or **trees**; neuter, third person, plural, Rule IX; nominative case, Rule I.

Their—pronoun, personal, simple, its antecedent is **birds**; neuter, third person, plural, Rule IX; possessisve, Rule III.

8. **He**—pronoun, personal, simple, its antecedent is the name, understood, of the person spoken of; masculine, third person, singular, Rule IX; nominative, Rule III.

Who—pronoun, relative, its antecedent is **rogue**; masculine, third person, singular, Rule IX; nominative, Rule I.

His (both uses)—pronoun, personal, simple, its antecedent is **rogue**; masculine, third person, singular, Rule IX; possessive, Rule III.

9. **Him**—pronoun, personal, simple, its antecedent is **Time**; masculine, third person, singular, Rule IX; objective, object of **can stay**, Rule VI.

His (both uses)—pronoun, personal, simple, its antecedent is **Time**; masculine, third person, singular, Rule IX; possessive case, Rule III.

221. ANTECEDENTS CONNECTED BY "AND"
EXERCISES

To be analyzed and parsed. Here follows a brief analysis of the pronoun usage in these exercises. Parsing is done as in the previous exercise, following rules on pages 42-50.

1. **Their**—plural required, since both boys are flying kites.

2. **Our**—plural required, since both should study.

3. **It**—singular required, since bread and milk are served as one dish; bread mixed with milk.

4. **His**—singular required, since **good man** is emphatically distinguished from **sinner** by the adverb **too**.

5. **His**—singular required, since **philosopher** and **statesman** are the same person.

6. **Them**—plural, since **horse** and **wagon** are distinguished by the article, **a**. (The animal and the vehicle were purchased and sold separately. But **horse and wagon**—a single rig—requires **it**.)

7. **Its**—singular; **house and lot** are a unit.

Page 161

222. ANTECEDENTS CONNECTED BY "OR" OR "NOR"
EXERCISES

To be corrected:

1. their (or, correct)
2. **George or Charles is diligent in his business**

(or, **in their business**, if a business in common is meant).

3. . . . **suffer for his opinion, he is a martyr.**

4. **him or her** (or, correct)

5. To retain the conjunction, **or**, in this sentence would result in an awkward sentence. Say, **Both poverty and wealth have their temptations**.

To be analyzed and parsed:

1. **His**—singular; the book will be borrowed from but one person.

2. **It**—singular; only one limb is to be amputated.

3. **Himself**—singular; Rule XI pertaining to **nor** so requires.

4. **Her**—singular; only one girl is expected to recite.

5. **Itself**—singular; Rule XI so requires; **rock** and **heath** are compared.

6. **His**—singular—James was wrong and his father right, or vice-versa—not both.

7. **Their**—plural; **students** is plural.

Page 162
EXERCISES

To be analyzed and parsed. Here follows a brief analysis of the usage of the adjectives and participles in these exercises. For parsing, see pages 30-39; 58-61.

1. **Birdlike** and **pure** are adjectives modifying **spirit**.

2. **Dim** and **cheerless**—adjectives, modify **scene**.

3. **This**—demonstrative, points to **life**. **Wild** and **Eolian**—adjectives, modify **harp**. **Many a** and **joyous**—adjectives, modify **strain**.

4. **Every**—adjective, modifies **treetop**.

5. **Fleecy**—adjective, modifies **clouds**. **Blanched**—past participle of the verb **blanch**; modifies **sky**.

6. **Primeval**—adjective, modifies **forest**.

7. **Impious**—adjective, modifies **it**. **A** and **good**—adjectives, modify **man**.

8. **Pious, brave,** and **wise**—adjectives, modify the subject infinitive **to hope the best**. **Best**—adjective, functions as the noun subject of **to hope**; it is modified by **the**, an article adjective.

9. **Wasted** and **used**—past participles of **waste** and **use**, modify the noun **time**.

10. **Shut**—past participle of the irregular verb, **shut**, modifies **thoughts**.

Unopened—adjective, modifies **bales**.

11. **An, empty**—adjectives, modify **dream**.

12. **Living**— participle noun/gerund, object of the preposition, **for**.

Terrible, strong—adjectives, modify **struggle**.

13. **Petulant**—adjective, modifies **she**.

Set—past participle of **set**, modifies **rosebud**.

Little, willful—adjectives, modify **thorns**.

Sweet—adjective, modifies **rosebud**.

English—proper adjective, modifies **air**.

14. **Dearest**—adjective, superlative of **dear**, modifies **hills**.

Childish—adjective, modifies **feet**.

The, most sweet—adjectives, modify **streams**; **most sweet** is the emphatic superlative of **sweet**.

Young—adjective, modifies **lips**.

Stoop'd—past participle of **stoop**, modifies **lips**.

Grassy—adjective, modifies **bank**.

15. **Narrow, stately**—adjectives, modify **walls** or **halls**.

Pages 163-164
224. VERBS
EXERCISES
To be corrected:
1. were
2. have been fed
3. were
4. helps
5. were
6. was (British, were)
7. was
8. has
9. are undividually (The members of the corporation are individually would be a better construction.)
10. is
11. are
12. is
13. derivation . . . is
14. board . . . has

Page 164
To be analyzed and parsed. Brief analyses given here; for parsing see pages 54-89, if the teacher feels the student needs this extra work.

1. **Came** and **went** are the verbs; **tomorrow**, subject.

2. **Return**, verb; **you**, understood, subject; **days**, noun of direct address in the objective case, is the antecedent of **return**.

3. **Was**, verb; **I**, subject.

4. **Deserves**, verb; **this**, subject.

5. **Arrive**, verb; **diligences**, subject.

6. **Waved**, verb; **he**, subject.

7. **Has**, verb; **creature**, subject.

8. **Needs**, verb; **present**, subject.

9. **Were**, verb; **jury**, subject.

10. **Passes**, verb; **generation** (first usage) subject.

PAGE 164-166

(**Generation**, second usage, is the object of the preposition **after**).

11. **Are** (or **is**), verb; **public**, subject.

12. **Bequeaths**, verb; **age**, subject.

13. **'s (is)**, verb; **there**, subject.

Makes, verb; **that**, understood, is the subject of this relative clause.

14. **Has** (after dash), verb of main clause; **he**, subject.

Attends, verb; **that** is the subject of the first relative clause; **he** is the antecedent of **that**.

Has and **keeps**, verb; **that**, subject of second relative clause; **he** is **that's** antecedent.

Hungers and **supplies**, verb; **that**, subject of the third relative clause; **he** is also its antecedent.

Has, verb; **he**, understood, subject of the second principal clause.

Seeks, verb of the fourth relative clause; **who**, subject; **he**, understood, its antecedent.

15. **Arose**, verb; **contest**, subject.

Set, verb; **spectacles**, subject.

Was, verb; **point**, subject.

Knows, verb; **world**, subject.

Ought, verb; **spectacles**, subject.

Page 165
SUBJECTS CONNECTED BY "AND"
EXERCISES
To be corrected:
1. were
2. wait
3. is (Use **are** with **Both bread and milk are good food.**)
4. knows
5. deserves
6. remove
7. is
8. have become
9. A number . . . was . . . .

To be analyzed and parsed:
1. **Beauty**, singular subject, is distinguished emphatically by **not**; singular verb, **attracts**, is required.

2. **Wife**, singular, distinguished emphatically by **no**; singular verb, **was**, is required.

3. **Proceed**, plural verb of **blessing and cursing**, subject. **Out of . . . mouth** is an adverbial prepositional phrase.

4. **You and I**, plural subject, requires the plural verb, **look**.

5. **Uncle**, singular subject, requires the singular verb, **is**. **With his wife** is a prepositional phrase modifying **uncle**.

6. **Charles and Emma**, plural subject, requires the plural verb, **are**.

7. **Charles**, singular subject, requires the singular verb, **is studying**. **Together with . . . Emma** is a prepositional phrase modifying **Charles**.

8. **Crime**, emphatically distinguished from **scaffold** by **not**, requires the singular verb **makes**.

9. The plural subject, **ambition and avarice**, requires the plural verb, **are**.

10. The plural subject, **fire, strength,** and **firmness**, requires the plural verb, **are**. The modifying phrases do not constitute emphatic distinction.

11. **A coach and six**, a unit, is a singular subject requiring the singular verb, **is**.

12. **Day**, singular subject, requires the singular verb, **is**. **An hour**, set off in commas, is an appositive.

Page 166
EXERCISES
To be corrected:
1. Have
2. Was
3. was
4. has been
5. is
6. am
7. are
8. cold . . . delays
9. moves
10. relatives
11. Not the . . . Cham of Tartary is in his house monarch more than I.

To be analyzed and parsed:
1. **She**, singular subject; **has spoken**, singular verb, required because the subject is joined by **or**.

2. **Or**, conjunction, joins the two infinitive-phrase subjects. **To betray . . .** requires the singular subject, **is**.

3-7 are all **or/nor** compound subjects; in all these cases the subject nearest the verb is singular or collective, requiring singular verbs, thus: **ambition was; revenge deserves; riches is; pride keeps; Jane has lost.**

8. The subject of this quote from Gray's "Elegy," **horn**, ordinarily requires a third person singular verb, since it is joined to the rest of the subject (**call, swallow, clarion**) by the conjunction **or**.

Shall rouse, the verb, however, though singular as well as plural, is second or third person; the usual first person singular form is **will rouse** (cf. page 76, **future tense**).

Gray has evidently chosen **shall** for two reasons: **Shall** is proper with the third person, as here, when determination is indicated. He has negated determination in this instance by modifying the verb with **no more**, showing the futility of expecting the dead to respond to morning calls. He has woven subtle alliteration into his verse with soft **s** and **l** combinations to highlight the romantic mood of his poem (**call, incense, breathing, swallow, straw-built shed, shrill clarion, shall**).

9. Two lines of prepositional phrases introduce the singular subject, **all**, requiring the singular verb, **is**. The subordinate clause contains a compound subject joined by **or**. Since the final element in the subject, **leaf**, is singular, the verb is singular—**is**.

10. The conjunction **nor** requires that the singular noun, **Eternity**, nearest the verb, determine its number. **Hath seen** is singular. (The plural is **have seen**.)

That which is, a noun clause, is the singular subject of the second principal clause of this compound-complex sentence and verse. **Hath been**, the verb, is third person, singular.

Page 167
EXERCISES
To be corrected:
1. He came to see us.
2. To eat one's dinner greedily . . . .
3. I dared him to come to me. [Rem. 5 does not apply, since **to come** here does not follow the verb, as an object (as, **He dare not (to) come**), but follows the object **him**.]
4. He dared not leave his room.
5. I saw him write in his book.
6. . . . to be tardy frequently.
7. He made his horses go very fast.
8. He needs to study . . . .
9. He need not remain long.
10. He intended to write you.
11. They had hoped to see you . . . .

Pages 167-168
To be analyzed and parsed:
1. **To do**, infinitive used as the subject, modified by **to do**, a predicate noun, in turn modified by the adjective clause, **that which is ordered to be done. To be done** is the object of the verb, **ordered**.
2. **To die**, subject; **to be banished**, predicate noun modifying the subject.
3. **To do**, with its compound object, **justice and judgement**, is the subject of the verb, **is**.
4. **To try** and **to succeed**, infinitives, are here adjectives modifying the nouns **duty** and **determination**, respectively.
5. **To think** is the object of the verb **had dared**.

6. **To be attended**, infinitive, modifies the predicate noun **curse**.

To break and **to understand**, infinitives.

7. **You**, understood, subject; **look**, verb, modified adverbially by **to see**, infinitive. (The construction is the same in both **look to see** clauses.)

Ye, subject; **call**, verb, modified adverbially by **to**, understood, **be answered**.

Pages 168-169
228. INFINITIVES NOT USED AS NOUNS
EXERCISES
To be parsed. Here follows partial analysis, necessary for parsing of these infinitives functioning as adjectives and adverbs. See also page 65, number 99.

1. **To talk**, adverb, modifies the verb **come**.
2. **To spin**, adverb, modifies **can see**.
3. **To be**, understood, joins the adjective **glad** to the noun **mortal**.

To be glad is an adjective infinitive phrase.

4. **To die** and **to live**, adverbs, modify the verbs **lived** and **died**, respectively.
5. **To understand**, adjective, modifies the noun, **thing**.
6. **Better**, predicate adjective modifying the subject, **it**, is adverbially modified by the infinitives **to fight** and **to rail**, joined by **than**, a conjunction.
7. **You**, understood, subject; **let**, verb; **us**, object. **(To) be content**, infinitive phrase, adjectively modifies the object, **us**; and **to do** and **to fret** adverbially modify the verb, **let**.
8. **To find a world**, infinitive phrase, modifies **time**, a predicate noun.
9. **To give true relish**, infinitive phrase, modifies the copula, **are**.
10. **You**, understood, subject of the main clause; **learn**, verb, modified by the adverbs **well** and **know**. **That** is the understood subject of the subordinate clause; **need**, its verb, modified adverbially by the infinitive **(to) be known**.
11. **You**, understood, subject; **let**, verb, modified adverbially by **(to) violate**.

You, understood, is the subject of the second principal clause; **own** (acknowledge), the verb; **man**, the object of **own**. **To live** and **(to) die**, adverbial infinitives, modify **born**, a participle adjective modifying **man**.

12. **To rouse** and **to start**, adverbs, modify the verb **stirs**.
13. **To mourn** and **to mend**, adverbs modify **lacks** (both uses), the verb.

Page 170
To be corrected:
   1. any satisfaction
   2. anybody
   3. Nobody ever or one never
   4. nor ever was more ungrateful
   5. smooth
   6. He speaks slowly and distinctly.
   7. beautiful
   8. splendidly
   9. tolerably
   10. scarcely
   11. more handsomely
   12. I want only to borrow ....
   13. to come in ... to go out
   14. almost
   15. I would not have believed anyone, or I would have believed no one.
   16. usually
   17. Our dog is usually ....
   18. Are you sometimes despondent?

To be analyzed and parsed:
   1. **Once more,** compound adverb modifying the copula, **was.** Or **once** may be parsed as the adverbial prepositional phrase **for once,** modified by **more.** In either case, the result is the same.
   2. **Therein,** obsolete adverb now supplanted by the adverbial phrase, **in this;** modifies the verb, **must minister,** also modified by **to himself.**
   3. **(To) sweep,** adverb, modifies **saw; along,** adverb, modifies **to sweep.**
   4. **Right,** adverb, and **over against our homes,** adverbial phrase, modify the verb, **erects.**
   5. **Slowly,** adverb, and **o'er the tomb-paved ground,** adverbial phrase, modify the verb, **moves.**
   6. **To be loved** and **to be lovely,** infinitives used as adverbs, modify the verb, **desire. Only,** adverb, modifies these phrases; and the adverb **not** modifies **only.**
   7. **Westward,** adverb, modifies the verb **takes.**
   8. **Not,** an adverb, modifies the verb **move.**
   9. **Dimly,** adverb, and **through the mists and vapors,** adverbial phrase, modify the verb **see.** But (only), adverb, modifies the adverb **dimly.**
   10. **Man by man, foot by foot,** and **over the Alps** are adverbial prepositional phrases modifying the verb, **did proceed. Man** and **foot,** first usage, may also be parsed as the objects of understood prepositions.
   11. **Already,** adverb, modifies **is begun;** either, adverb, modifies **must conquer or perish,** the verb.
   12. **Up,** adverb, modifies **heaped; miserably,** adverb, modifies **passed.**
   13. **Out,** adverb, modifies **are burnt; tiptoe** and the phrase **on top,** adverbs, modify the verb **stands.**
   14. **More,** adverb, modifies the verb **I'll look; more** is modified by the adverb **no. Down headlong,** compound adverb, modifies the verb **topple.**
   15. **We,** subject; **kept,** verb; **pace,** object. **Changing,** a participle, modifies **we; never,** adverb, modifies **changing.**
   The adverbial prepositional phrases **(with) not a word, neck by neck,** and **stride by stride** modify the verb **kept. To each other,** an adjective phrase, modifies **word,** object of **with,** understood.
   16. **Breath,** subject; **is,** verb; **agitation,** predicate noun in the first clause. **Life,** subject of the second principal clause; **is,** understood, its verb; **storm,** predicate noun.
   Whereon, a relative pronoun, introduces the adjective clause, **they ride,** which modifies **storm. To sink,** adverbial infinitive, modifies the verb, **ride;** and the phrase **at last** modifies **to sink.**
   17. **Who,** subject of the first adjective clause; **does,** the verb; **best,** the object. **Circumstance** is the subject of the second adjective clause modifying **best; allows** is its verb.
   He, understood, is the subject of the main clause, modified by **who does.** Its verb is **does** (and) **acts** (second line), modified by the adverbs **well** and **nobly. Angels,** subject, and **could (do),** verb, comprise the second main clause. **More,** adverb, modifies **could do; no** modifies **more.**
   Act, subject; **admits,** verb; **restraint,** object. **Indeed,** a modal adverb, modifies this entire clause.
   'T (it), subject; **is,** verb, modified by the infinitive adverb, **to domineer,** in turn modified by the adverbial phrase, **in things. Over thought,** an adjective phrase, modifies **things.**
   You, understood, subject; **guard,** verb; **well,** adverb modifying **guard.**
   Thoughts, subject; **are heard,** verb, modified by the adverbial phrase, **in heaven.**

230. PREPOSITIONS
EXERCISES
To be corrected, if necessary, and parsed. The teacher should here refer to Section 140, "Caution," pages 98-99.
   1. **Upon**—preposition, shows the relation between **relatives** and **is dependent,** Rule XIX.
   2. **From**—shows the relation between **you** and **differ.**
   On—shows the relation between **point** and **differ.**
   3. **With**—shows the relation between **sword** and **was killed.**
   By—shows the relation between **violence** and **died.**

4. **Between**—shows the relation between **them** and **divided**.

5. **In**—shows the relation between **lifetime** and **was shipwrecked**.

6. **Above**—shows the relation between **rage** and **watched**. (This is a tricky one, given away by the possessive use of **tempests'**. **Tempests** and **clouds** are used here adjectively as a compound possessive to modify **rage**, the object of the preposition.)

Across—shows the relation between **arch** and **watched**.

Upon—shows the relation between **pilgrimage** and **watched**.

Page 172
213. COORDINATE CONJUNCTIONS
EXERCISES
To be corrected and parsed:

1. We moved along silently and cautiously.
2. To play is more pleasant than to work, **or,** Playing is more pleasant than working.
3. They either could not learn, or they desired not to do so.
4. He can brag of past accomplishments, but he is no longer able to do much (**answers will vary**).
5. That lot is preferable to yours, and it is cheaper.
6. He looks sad though he is hungry.
7. He has neither love nor veneration for him.
8. I cannot tell whether or not he has returned.
9. Neither James nor John came home yesterday.
10. I always desire your society, and I always wish for it.
11. The boy would have his own way, and he did.
12. The parliament addressed the king and adjourned its session the same day.

Page 173
232. SUBORDINATE CONJUNCTIONS
EXERCISES
To be parsed:

1. **That**—subordinate conjunction; connects **thought** and **it could be so**.
2. **After (that)**—conjunction; connects **locks** and **the horse is stolen**.
3. **Why**—conjunctive adverb; joins **know** and **you deceived me**.
4. **Wherever**—conjunction, joins **he may be** to **he will have friends**.
5. **However**—joins **he may seem stern** to **he is a good man. However** is here a conjunctive adverb.
6. **While**—conjunction; joins **there is life** to **there is hope**.

7. **For**—conjunction; joins **blessed are the merciful** to **they shall obtain mercy**.
8. **As if**—compound conjunction; joins **rushes** to **he were summoned to a banquet**.
9. **Whether**—conjunction; joins the noun clause subject, **the planets are inhabited** to its verb, **was discussed**.
10. **Where**—conjunction; joins the noun clause object, **he is** to the verb, **do know**.
11. **That**—conjunction; joins **there was so much noise** to **I could not sleep**.
12. **Though**—conjunction; joins **we part in sorrow** to **we meet**.

But—conjunction; joins **we meet tomorrow** to **we part**.

233. INTERJECTIONS
To be parsed. All the interjections in this exercise denote strong emotion and have no dependence upon other words, Rule XXII. See pages 103-104, Sections 148-151.

1. **What!**
2. **Ha!**
3. **Ho, warden!**
4. **Oh, fearful woe!**
5. **Ah!**
6. **Ouch!**
7. **Hark! Hark!**
8. **Halloo, my boys, halloo!**
9. **Pshaw!**
10. **Oh, look!**
11. **Aha!**
12. **Alas, poor Yorick!**
13. **Adieu, adieu, my native land!**
14. **Hark!**

Page 179
236. EXERCISES

(With this grammar course coming to a close, the teacher may wish to use these 56 exercises for review of several earlier sections.)

Page 190
EXERCISES
Insert commas wherever required:

1. Come, Rover –
2. commend, as well as censure,
3. poor, the high and the low,
4. I see, then, in revelation,
5. Oranges, lemons,
6. think, John, Paul asked at last,
7. Yes,
8. then, so
9. seeketh, findeth
10. indolent, power

Page 191
EXERCISES
Insert commas and semicolons:

   1. shower, and . . . a flood, and a flood a storm, and a storm a tempest, and . . . lightning, and . . . .

   2. abrupt, darting, scornful . . . face; humor . . . shy, ...

   3. readily; otherwise . . . .

   4. sandwiches, cake, and cookies; Tom . . . .

Page 192
EXERCISES
Insert colons:

   1. senses: sight   3. brass: their

   2. parts: in   4. example: the

Page 193
EXERCISES
Insert periods:

   1. D. K. Merwin, Esq. was chosen chairman.

   2. H. C. Cartwright. b. A.D. 1825, d. Feb. 2, 1854.

   3. See Rev. 12:11.

   4. Chapter XXIV. Part II.

   5. It cost $10.22.

Page 194
EXERCISES
Insert the punctuation required.

   1. What did my father's godson seek? Your life? He whom my father named?

   2. See, there! Look!

Page 196
EXERCISES
Insert the dash and parentheses:

   1. head—his . . . any night—a tooth . . . .

   2. Of duty—the most . . . .

   3. architecture (see Dr. Pocock, not his discourses but his prints)

Page 198
Punctuate properly the following examples: (Answers may vary):

"What, Tubero, did that naked sword of yours mean in the Battle of Pharsalia? At whose breast was its point aimed? What was then the meaning of your arms, your spirit, your eyes, your ardor of soul? What did you desire—what wish for?"

"I press the youth too much. He seems disturbed. Let me return to myself. I, too, bore arms on the same side."—*Cicero*.

"Presently my soul grew stronger; hesitating then no longer,
'Sir,' said I, 'or Madam, truly your forgiveness I implore;
But the fact is, I was napping, and so gently you came rapping,
And so faintly you came tapping, tapping at my chamber door,
That I scarce was sure I heard you'—here I opened wide the door—
   Darkness there, and nothing more."—*Poe*.

Pages 208-209
263. SCANNING
EXERCISES

Here we have done the first and seventh examples. Students can do the others by referring to pages 202-207.

   1. Sweet day´! | so cool´, | so calm´, | so bright´,
     ´ The bri´ | dal of´ | the earth´ | the sky´;
    The dews´ | shall weep´ | thy fall´ | tonight´;
      For thou´ | must die´.—*Herbert*.

   7. Thou art´— | direct´ | ing, guid´ | ing all´— | Thou art´!
     Direct´ | my un´ | derstand´ | ing, then´, | to Thee´;
    Control´ | my spir´ | it, guide´ | my wan´ | d'ring heart´,
     Though but´ | an at´ | om midst´ | immen´ | sity´,
    Still I´ | am some´ | thing fash´ | ioned by´ | thy hand´!
     I hold´ | a midd´ | le rank´ | 'twixt heav'n´ | and earth´,
    On the´ | last verge´ | of mor´ | tal be´ | ing stand´,
     Close to´ | the realms´ | where an´ | gels have´ | their birth´,
    Just on´ | the boun´ | d'ries of´ | the spir´ | it land´.—*Derzhaven*